THE SPIRITUAL DOCTRINE
OF
DOM MARMION

THE SPIRITUAL DOCTRINE

OF

DOM MARMION

BY

M. M. PHILIPON, O.P., M.S.T.

Translated by

Dom MATTHEW DILLON
Monk of Glenstal Priory

THE NEWMAN PRESS
Westminster, Maryland

Nihil Obstat: JOANNES M. T. BARTON, S.T.D., L.S.S.
CENSOR DEPUTATUS

Imprimatur: E.MORROGH BERNARD.
VIC. GEN.

Westmonasterii, die 27a Junii, 1956.

Imprimi Potest: 22nd March, 1956. D. PLACID MURRAY, O.S.B.
PRIOR

DECLARATION

MADE AND PRINTED IN GREAT BRITAIN
BY NORTHUMBERLAND PRESS LIMITED
GATESHEAD ON TYNE

CONTENTS

5

Part IV

SACERDOS ALTER CHRISTUS

1. CHRIST, A PRIEST FOR EVER

2. THE PRIESTHOOD IN THE CHURCH

8 *Contents*

Part V

THE MOTHER OF CHRIST

Epilogue

PREFACE

I T may perhaps seem surprising that a son of St. Dominic should undertake a meticulous study of the spiritual doctrine of a son of St. Benedict. The explanation is that Father Philipon appreciated the outstanding importance of Dom Marmion's work in Christian spirituality. It appeared to him that Dom Marmion ranked with Sister Elizabeth of the Trinity and St. Thérèsa of Lisieux as a teacher designed by Providence to re-establish in our times some of the most fundamental themes of the Gospel. He believed, and rightly, that a clear exposition of the main points of his salutary teaching would be supremely useful to souls.

It is a pleasure to acknowledge the professional care with which the work has been carried out. The author's critical sense impelled him to go to the original sources for his information, and he made a careful study of all the manuscripts which Dom Marmion left us. From these he has extracted the essence of his spiritual teaching. Moreover, I am happy to say that he has been completely successful in his efforts to enter into the Benedictine mentality as Dom Marmion understood it.

The spiritual doctrine of Dom Marmion is in the fullest accord with the teaching of the Church, but it needed the learning of a theologian to bring out the full power of his teaching.

Finally, his wide knowledge of asceticism and mysticism together with his experience of souls has enabled Father Philipon to appreciate and to reveal how completely Dom Marmion's doctrine depended on the intensity of his own inner life.

In this book we have a sober personal exposition by a master of the noble and original teaching of another master.

DOM R. THIBAUT.

INTRODUCTION

In writing the history of spirituality in the twentieth century it is natural to begin with Dom Marmion. His work initiated a profound spiritual revival the influence of which has permeated the whole Catholic world. It is to him that we owe in great measure this return to that primary truth of the Christian faith: Christ, the model and sole source of life for us. He had some admirable precursors in this revival of Christo-centric religion: Scheeben in German-speaking countries, Fr. Faber in England, Mgr. Gay, steeped in the teaching of the French School; but none of these attained his world-wide influence.

The publication of *Christ, the Life of the Soul* (1917) marks the opening of a new era in spirituality, inaugurating as it did the celebrated trilogy which was completed by *Christ in His Mysteries* (1919), and *Christ the Ideal of the Monk* in 1922. *Christ the Ideal of the Priest*, published posthumously in 1951, is the final consummation of his work.

The prodigious and unexpected success of *Christ the Life of the Soul*, showed clearly to what an extent this form of spirituality, steeped in dogma, simple, stripped of all that was accidental and centred on Christ, corresponded to the secret longing of the Christian conscience. It was like "a revelation of truths forgotten."[1]

Christian souls were at last re-discovering their Master. They never tired of reading and re-reading these pregnant, vigorous pages in which Christ was presented to them as the model and life-giving source of all sanctity, inviting us to die to sin so that we might live only in Him, to unite ourselves with the Church in her praise of the Word Incarnate and to

---

[1] Dom Marmion, passing through Paris, wrote to Dom Thibaut on March 2nd, 1919: "I am more and more astonished at the reception accorded to the first volume. Wherever I go it is the same thing. They tell me that it is like a revelation of truths forgotten."

allow ourselves to be led by Him " to the bosom of the Father."

These fundamental ideas, which have become familiar to us, caused a sensation at the time, giving as they did a definite orientation to Catholic spirituality, not by way of novelty but as a re-assertion of the predominance of Christ in our lives. It was the providential mission of Dom Marmion to re-establish the person of Christ as the fountain head of modern spirituality. It was a revolution effected by a return to what was fundamental. The public received with the same enthusiasm the letters of direction of the Abbot of Maredsous, and his biography written by the masterly hand of Dom Thibaut with the precision of an historian and the feeling of a devoted son. It is to him that we owe the *" Corpus asceticum"* of Dom Marmion. The Abbot of Maredsous, replying to the congratulations of a correspondent, writes humorously: " I have not even a temptation to vanity, for I have no part in it. It is Christ and St. Paul who speak, and one of my monks has edited their text. My only contribution is my name on the cover. All the same, Christ is so generous that He will give me credit for having wished to make Him loved."[2]

In fact it is Christ and St. Paul who speak through the soul of Dom Marmion. The genius of Dom Thibaut has collected the product of this fountain of wisdom and transmitted it to us with admirable fidelity.

Providence had prepared him ideally for the task. Having entered Maredsous on October 1st, 1890 at the age of nineteen, Dom Raymond Thibaut in the first twenty years of his monastic life was first pupil, then under the spiritual direction of Dom Marmion. Later he was his monk, an attentive assistant at his conferences, and finally, in the years when the trilogy was in course of preparation, the trustee and confidant of the noble spiritual concepts of the Abbot of Maredsous.

It would be impossible to find anyone better suited to such a work than Dom Thibaut, who combined the positive mind of a professional historian with the experience of a professor and a director of a review, to which may be added his inherent intellectual qualities, his habit of work and his zeal for clarity

[2] Letter to Winefrid Kraemer, Maredsous, October 6th, 1920.

and precision. The Prior of Maredsous chose him for the task. Dom Thibaut accepted it in the spirit of obedience. He set to work collating his texts, harmonizing them and restoring their spiritual setting.

After much labour, he went to submit the results of his efforts to the convent of Maredret, which had collected and committed to writing the greater part of the retreats and conferences of Dom Marmion. The reaction was immediate. "These are the ideas of Father Abbot but you have not recaptured his living, spontaneous style, direct and overflowing in its enthusiasm for Christ". Dom Thibaut humbly laid aside the five hundred pages already written and looked at them no more. Beginning the work again he executed it methodically, submitting it chapter by chapter to the nuns at Maredret, particularly qualified as they were by their familiarity with Dom Marmion as *conférencier* to pass judgement on the work. Thus was born *Christ the Life of the Soul* which was destined to spread throughout the world. The other books were compiled under the same conditions with scrupulous exactitude and constant recourse to the judgement of Dom Marmion himself, who approved, amended, and made additions, sometimes with his own hand—especially in *Christ in His Mysteries*—of new developments of his thought.

This control confers on the whole work the true personal seal of authenticity. Dom Thibaut for his part has succeeded in reproducing the thought of his Abbot with all the force and skill of an ear-witness. The trilogy is therefore the lasting expression of the doctrine and spirit of Dom Marmion and the principal source of his teaching to which we must always return. The posthumous work, *Christ the Ideal of the Priest*, which could not be subjected to this personal control, is none the less authentic, having been compiled with the same scrupulous objectivity and with the assistance of numerous autograph manuscripts. Dom Thibaut has given us a definitive work. It is the work of a great master of the spiritual life which has been given to us. Dom Marmion follows in the purest line of the Benedictine tradition. The Rule of St. Benedict was imprinted on his soul. As soon as he entered the monastery Dom Columba began to study it eagerly. All the rest of his life he was commenting on it, as Prior of Mont César at Louvain or as Abbot of Maredsous, from the spiritual rather than the scholarly point of view, seeking in this venerable text, which has formed thousands and thousands of saints, the secret of practising a similar heroic virtue, and lost in wonder at the simplicity of Christian perfection in the School of St. Benedict.

"I am profoundly convinced that the doctrine of our holy Father, full as it is of the spirit of the Gospel, can lead men to the highest degree of perfection that can be attained on this earth."[3]

The exposition of his own spiritual doctrine is everywhere reminiscent of the rule or of the developments inspired by it. He draws from it the fundamental themes of his conferences and retreats: humility, compunction of heart, his sense of monastic obedience extending to the attempting of the impossible but always in the spirit of love, the primary importance of the Opus Dei and that incessant quest of God which is the inspiration of the whole Benedictine rule and the one object of the monastic life; and finally this theo-centrism which, freeing the soul from its trammels, preserves it constantly in the presence of God and makes it forget itself in the simplicity, the discretion and self-dedication of the children of God. He appreciated the spiritual genius of St. Benedict who had succeeded right from the Prologue of the Rule in "entering into the spirit of the Divine Plan and referring all things to God through Christ,[4] putting at our disposal the immense riches of the Christian faith."[5] He loved those maxims and counsels which prescribed living familiarly in the presence of Christ "loved above all things and preferred to all things". The *Nihil amori Christi praeponere* seemed to him to be the culmination of the Benedictine rule and the final expression of its spirit. *Christ the Ideal of the Monk* is radiant with this concept and portrays for us the intimate religious life of Dom Marmion. It was in this living framework of Benedictine monasticism that he

[3] Retreat Maredret, December 1905.
[4] Ibidem.
[5] Conference, Maredret, July 15th, 1914.

evolved his own teaching based on the most fundamental sources of the Christian faith: Holy Scripture and the Sacred Sciences.

He was devoted to the Bible, the whole Bible, advising that it be read in its entirety. He saw in the Old Testament the key to the New; for, as he remarked, there is no break of continuity in the works of God.[6]

But of the inspired authors it was undoubtedly St. Paul who had the most profound influence on him. He had his writings always at hand. He liked to read them in the Greek. He did not approve of contenting oneself with a few verses; he recommended the reading of a whole epistle at a time. Thus the thought of the Apostle was revealed to him in its grandiose perspective as vast as the redemption itself and the mystery of Christ was shown to him in all its immensity as the very centre of the plan of salvation according to the eternal decrees of the divine plan.

From this reading his contemplative soul derived a profound understanding of the rôle of Christ in the life of the soul: a predestination to adoptive Sonship imaged in the Divine Son, the universality of the Saviour whom God gave us to be "our wisdom, our justification, our redemption and all our sanctity."[7]

Hence the appreciation of our wretchedness as sinners and of our weakness, but also of our infinite richness in Jesus Christ and that intuitive understanding of all Christian mysticism, of death and of life, unto the final antithesis: "I live now, not I but Christ liveth in me."[8]

All these great Pauline theses were assimilated by Dom Marmion and incorporated in his own thought which became almost indistinguishable from that of the Apostle. Dom Marmion looked on Christ through the eyes of St. Paul.

If the principal theses of the doctrine of the Abbot of Maredsous are inspired by St. Paul, they are given expression in accordance with the classical theological tradition. Dom Marmion searches the Scriptures and follows closely the

[6] Conference, Maredret, March 4th, 1910.
[7] I Cor. 1.30.
[8] Gal. ii, 20.

declarations of the Councils and the writings of the great masters of the Church. He has read St. Augustine, Saint Gregory, and St. Bernard, whose commentary on the Canticle of Canticles aroused his special enthusiasm.[9] Taking a text of the great doctor (Bernard), Dom Marmion gave a commentary on it to the Benedictines of Maredret in a series of conferences which form the substance of *Sponsa Verbi, the Virgin consecrated to Christ.* He was familiar with the great spiritual writers of the Benedictine Order, especially Blosius.[10] The Chapters of St. Francis de Sales on holy abandonment in his "Treatise on the love of God" confirmed and enriched his own concept.

In his readings and appreciations he employed a wide and balanced eclecticism, but in Theology St. Thomas Aquinas was the guide of his thought. With the Bible and the Liturgy, the *Summa Theologica* was his constant companion. He meditated on it continually in order to draw from it new lights on the mysteries of God. He recommends it for assiduous reading: "Try to deepen your understanding of St. Thomas, he has so much to give.[11] He studied him sometimes on his knees; and after his lectures some of his students would move spontaneously to the choir to continue their meditation of the divine mysteries which he had developed in his teaching.[12]

For him Theology was in fact "the evolution of faith in prayer"[13] From this Sacred Science he seeks above all else to be enabled to reach God through love. In this regard nothing can be more significant than his private notes as a young professor of theology, which are so revealing of the outlook which he maintained to the end of his life: "For the last few months I have been teaching the treatise *de Deo Uno.* I have received much light on the divine Nature. While meditating on the words "*Ego sum qui sum*", I saw that our duties to God are all comprised in adoration. Faith is the adoration of God considered as *Summa Veritas*; hope as

---

[9] Retreat, Maredsous, September 1919.
[10] Monastic conferences Maredret, October 15th, 1909.
[11] Letter of August 5th, 1902.
[12] Cf. *A Master of the Spiritual Life*, p. 146.
[13] Letter to the Abbess of Maredret, January 2nd, 1902.

everything in Jesus and through Him. He is the "Way" which the Father has given us, it is by Him that we must go. When I try to make my mental prayer in the "void", putting aside all the beautiful words, images and comparisons which Jesus used in His teaching, I am paralysed."[17]   God calls us in different ways. This is no reflection on the transcendent grandeur of the mystical genius of St. John of the Cross. For Dom Marmion Christ was the centre of everything. At his last priests' retreat in 1922 in the diocese of Tournai, he said to the priests confidentially by way of a final declaration of faith: "For my part, my whole spiritual life consists in Jesus Christ."[18]   All the mystical graces which he received converged towards this transformation into Christ which he desired to be complete to the point of identification: *Iam non ego, vivit vero in me Christus.*[19]   God, who had destined him to recall to His Church the "unfathomable riches of Christ,"[20] began by bringing to realization in him this programme of sanctity. As with the great mystics, his spiritual work is the supreme expression of his personal life.[21]

Certain characteristic notes of his doctrine are developed as a result of his experience and especially that fundamental trait of his spiritual outlook: his Christo-centrism. "In modern devotion", he used to say sadly, "Christ is not the ALL. The more I read Holy Scripture, the more I live the liturgy, the more clearly I see that one thought reigns supreme: Christ is the very centre of Creation."[22]   "Instead of conforming to the wisdom of the divine plan, men try to constitute themselves the architects of their own perfection,[23] substituting their human, petty concept for the divine thought." For his part he never ceased to be the apostle of the divine plan and

---

[17] Letter to a Carmelite nun, Beauplateau, September 25th, 1918.

[18] Priests' retreat, Tournai, August 1922.

[19] Gal. ii, 20.

[20] Eph. iii, 8.

[21] Cf. in *Presence de Dom Marmion* Desclee de Brouwer 1948, pp. 109-133. the remarkable study by Dom Ryelandt, an intimate friend of Dom Marmion and Dom Thibaut's colloborator in the preparation of *Christ the Ideal of the Priest.* Cf. the special number of *La Vie Spirituelle* devoted to Dom Marmion, January 1948.

[22] Monastic conferences, Maredret, April 22nd, 1914.

[23] Retreat Erdington, November 1902.

Introduction

Summa Fidelitas et Potentia; Charity as *Summa Bonitas,*
mission as *Summa Maiestas,* and as in God all these are
one being, adoration contains in radice these multiple act
So, for this contemplative monk, the study of theology alw,
culminated in adoration. All the treatises which he taug
were for him sources of vital illumination and showed him t
ways of God in the direction of souls. The treatise *De Ver*
Incarnato was always his favourite course, the one into whi
he penetrated most deeply. In it we see the inspiration
his masterpiece of spirituality. He drew also abundantly o
the doctrinal riches of the liturgy. Through it his soul rise
effortlessly to the highest contemplation of the divine
mysteries. Viewed in an atmosphere of prayer and by a light
from on high, it reproduces for him the dogmas of faith which
he has just taught. Above all, he finds in it Christ living in
His Church. The acts and gestures of the Saviour are not for
him a mere memorial of a distant past. The virtue of the
liturgy consists in perpetuating these mysteries among men
and thus applying to them the redemptive merits of Christ.
While the Voice of the Church, "Vox sponsae"[15] is united in
the praise of the Word Incarnate, a grace corresponding to
each of these mysteries is infused into the souls of those assisting, in proportion to their fervour and their faith. The liturgy
was for him "the most suitable food for the soul."[16] *Christ*
in His Mysteries bears testimony to this intimate conviction.

We have here the primary source of his doctrine: his personal perception of God in Christ. Herein lies the fundamental secret which explains the genius of this master of
spirituality. More than all his reading, it is love which has
revealed Christ to him. Dom Marmion the mystic does not
resemble St. John of the Cross. He admires the sublime
doctrine of the doctor of "the nights" and of the living flame
of love, but his own interior life was oriented in another
sense: "I have read St. John of the Cross attentively. His
writings are not suited to my soul. They take from me my
liberty in my dealings with God. My inclination is to find

[14] *Private Notes,* December 1891.
[15] *Private Notes,* May 1887.
[16] Conference Maredret, March 4th, 1910.

B

to preach Christ untiringly. "Do not weary of hearing me repeating the same truths. St. Paul, who had been raised to the third heaven and who had been privileged to see marvels which the mind of man cannot even conceive, spoke of nothing else but Jesus Christ and referred all things to Christ. *Praedestinavit nos conformes fieri imaginis Filii Sui.*[24] "He has predestined us to be moulded into the image of His Son." Read his epistles and you will see that this is the dominant idea ".[25]

The Abbot of Maredsous had met with a great number of souls "narrow, tormented, troubled" who were entirely introverted and had been taken out of themselves and restored to stable peace of heart by the sudden introduction of Christ into their lives.

It was the special grace of Dom Marmion to reveal Christ to souls and to concentrate them on Him. His written work, perpetuating the influence of his preaching, is exclusively directed to this end: "I have tried to show that Christian perfection consists simply in the domination of all our activity by Christ."[26]

As Christ is the centre of his spiritual teaching it follows that it is essentially dogmatic in character. His conferences and retreats are adorned with expositions of the principal mysteries of our faith. In a contemplative environment, in which he felt most at home, he often rose to great mystical heights of dogma while treating familiar subjects. The Son led him "to the bosom of the Father", where he liked to dwell on the generation of the Word and on the union of love between the Father and the Son from which the Holy Ghost proceeds. He liked to return to the mystery of the Incarnation as being the centre-point of his thought and would analyse at length the union of the two natures in Jesus Christ, His sanctity, His virtues and the operation of the gifts of the Holy Ghost in the soul of the Son.

This contemplation of the Word Incarnate led him to the

---

[24] Rom. viii, 29.
[25] Monastic conferences, Maredret, October 1909.
[26] To Dom Thibaut on the occasion of the publication of the last volume of the trilogy: *Christ the Ideal of the Monk.*

consideration of all the aspects of Theology, dogmatic and moral. Christ appeared to him as the living link between all the Christian mysteries. He is the focal point from which he contemplates the whole universe.

The synthesis which he worked out during a long life of teaching springs from an ardent contemplation of Christ. As dogma is the habitual food of his soul he considers everything from the spiritual point of view. Hence the grandeur of his concept of our Christian life which he sees as an "acceptance of the Incarnation,"[27] as a flowing of the divine life from the Father to the Son and from Him, through His Humanity and under the impulse of the Holy Spirit, into His Church and to each of the members of His Mystical Body. For Dom Marmion ascetic theology is closely connected with dogma and partakes of its sublimity. There is no fragmentation of our life: everything is reduced to unity.

Under the influence of the gifts of understanding and of wisdom he experienced this truth: "We are ONE with Christ and all the members of His Mystical Body. I am more and more convinced of it. Not only do I believe it; I *see* it."[28] For him the whole Catholic dogma shone forth in Christ.

His vigorous Christo-centrism freed him from all trace of narrow individualism and this is the explanation of a final characteristic of his work; its catholicity. The spirituality of Dom Marmion is developed in the atmosphere of the Church. In it the soul is never regarded as an individual alone with itself, concerned only with its own sanctification. It lives in communion with the whole mystical body without any exclusiveness, excepting no one, in the purest tradition of the Gospel and of St. Paul, considering nothing as foreign to it which regards Christ, the glory of the Father, or the attainment of salvation by all. Its horizons are immense, corresponding, so to speak, with the viewpoint of Christ Himself. This explains why all schools of spirituality feel at home in the teaching of Dom Marmion. Even when he is speaking to monks and priests, the Abbot of Maredsous is understood and appreciated by simple Christians. The living presence

[27] Priest's retreat, Louvain, November 1901.
[28] Retreat Maredret, December 1921.

of Christ in every page of his writings has effected this miracle
of catholicity.

The works of Dom Marmion may be reckoned henceforth
among the spiritual classics.

I confess that I have undertaken this work only after much
hesitation.

On the death of Dom Marmion there was found a considerable volume of manuscripts: his courses of dogmatic theology,
of Scripture, innumerable notes in his own handwriting,
schemes for his conferences to priests, for some of his retreats,
for various sermons; some notes relating to matters of great
importance, and finally a variety of personal notes and reflec-
tions written in note books, on loose pages, sometimes even in
pocket diaries. In addition to these records there were about
500 letters which Dom Thibaut had collected.

There is another series of documents still more revealing
of his outlook which permit us to grasp his thought in its
full vigour, in its first spontaneity, now figurative, now strictly
practical, or suddenly rising to magnificent heights of
mysticism: these are the reports of his retreats and conferences. These are not literal transcriptions but careful notes
taken by his hearers as he spoke. Although we get a very different style according as these notes come from Louvain,
Maredsous, Maredret, Jupille, etc., this does not affect the
substance of the thought, which has been carefully noted with
the utmost possible verbal exactitude. Amongst these the
notes of Maredret, which are confirmed by a veritable team
of scribes all well accustomed to the style of the Abbot, have
a special value.

I would like here to express my gratitude for the trust and
generosity with which all the documents have been put at my
disposal. It has enabled me to carry out the work with that
objectivity which only a constant recourse to the sources can
make possible. The difficulty lay in restoring to these documents that breath of life which had animated them. I always
recall the constantly repeated advice of our old master, le
père Lagrange, to restore texts to their proper setting. Before
beginning the work it seemed to me essential to have some
experience of the Benedictine life. I undertook therefore

retreats in a number of Benedictine monasteries in order to enter into the Benedictine mentality. The retreats which I conducted at Maredsous and Maredret gave me a great deal of valuable insight. I spoke with many monks who had known Dom Marmion. I learned much from souls whom he had directed. I tried to develop in myself the Benedictine spirit so that I might achieve an understanding of the Benedictine ideal which is one of the highest forms of Christian perfection.

I then began a careful study of the documents, extracting what seemed the most typical quotations and putting them in their natural setting. My object was to grasp the sources of inspiration of this living synthesis, based rather on personal experience than on abstract theory, and to avoid everything in the nature of an artificial setting or subjective reconstruction.

As I was dealing with a theologian who in general had given a clear exposition of his thought, it was sufficient to fit the texts into their psychological context in accordance with their inherent dynamism. To put them in any other setting would have been to alter fatally the original trend of Dom Marmion's thought. A soul is a universe which can only be understood from within in the complexity of its whole personality. It is essential to efface oneself.

After many years of painstaking research and of constant application to the texts of Dom Marmion, I received one impression standing out unmistakably: Christ was the great passion of his life.

I shall never forget the conviction of Mme. Cecile de Hemptinne, the Abbess foundress of Maredret, who was on terms of exceptional intimacy with Dom Marmion, when she said to me one day, " He had a real passion for Christ." Here we have the secret, the unique driving power which made him one of the greatest of the spiritual masters of our time.

Saint Maximin, January 25th, 1953, on the feast of the conversion of St. Paul.

I

POSSESSION OF A SOUL BY CHRIST

1. FORMATIVE PERIOD

Priestly formation: Irish faith – Holy Cross College – Rome –
Curate at Dundrum – Professor of Philosophy

Monastic formation: Benedictine vocation – Novitiate –
Solemn Profession – Monastic work – Interior life

2. SPIRITUAL DEVELOPMENT

Prior of Mont-César – Relations with the
outside world – Tendency towards identification with Christ

3. FINAL TRANSFORMATION IN CHRIST

Abbot of Maredsous – World-wide
influence – Consummation in Christ

"For me Jesus is Everything"
(*Dom Marmion*)

I

POSSESSION OF A SOUL
BY CHRIST

Dom Marmion was a saint of the Irish school. His rich personality concealed an intense interior life which drew its strength from a profound faith and an ardent, dominating passion for the adorable person of Christ. One of the monks who was closest to him declared: "He had his faults, but for Christ he would have done anything." The rising curve of this interior life corresponded to the progressive possession of his soul by Christ.

1. FORMATIVE PERIOD

PRIESTLY FORMATION

Irish Faith

Born in Dublin on Holy Thursday, April 1st, 1858, Joseph Marmion received on April 6th in the Church of St. Paul that grace of adoption of which he was later to be the theologian and the doctor. This spark of the divine life which he received in baptism developed in an outstandingly Christian atmosphere. The Marmion household was a flourishing centre of the well-known Irish faith.

When the son, with the eager zeal of a young seminarist, advised his father to practise the exercise of the presence of God, the latter, who was a splendid Catholic, replied: "My child, in the midst of my daily occupations I never let many minutes go by without making to God the offering of my whole being."[1] Dom Thibaut remarks with justice: "He owes to his Celtic origin his penetrating intelligence, his lively imagination, his sensibility, his exuberance and his youthful spirit. The French blood which ran in his veins contributes his clearness of mind, his habit of clear perception, his ease of exposition, and his uprightness of character. From the combination of the two he derives his constant gaiety and his generosity of heart with all the strength, devotion, and fine feeling which this noble quality implies."

His mother belonged to a family which originated in Lorraine and was firmly rooted in the Catholic faith. In the Marmion home, which was to produce nine children, four girls and five boys, everything was inspired by a living faith: prayers and other devotional exercises in common, daily Mass, frequent Communions, family festivals. Joseph was particularly attached to his sister, Rosie, his elder by three years, who was his confidante and his support in times of difficulty. Both were called to great heights of religious perfection.

One can imagine the profound effect that this early home education had on the soul of Dom Marmion. His formation was completed by his early lessons with the Augustinians and his secondary studies under the Jesuit fathers.[2]

In this atmosphere of Christian fervour Joseph's mind soon turned towards the idea of the priesthood, which was in full accord with the desires of his family and especially of his father. But on the eve of his entry to the seminary of Holy Cross a spiritual crisis very nearly deflected him for ever. After a tense interior struggle he came home in the evening triumphant and confided to his sister Rosie: "I was terribly tempted and thought of giving up the idea of entering the seminary. You must have prayed and prayed well for me." That day Joe Marmion's destiny was decided.

---

[1] For all this period see *A master of the Spiritual Life, Dom Columba Marmion.*

[2] He had his first lessons in a day school conducted by the Augustinians dedicated to St. Laurence O'Toole. At the age of ten he entered Belvedere College under the Jesuits and remained there from 1868 to 1874.

Holy Cross College

In January 1874, he entered the seminary of Holy Cross, Clonliffe, on the outskirts of Dublin, and found there a community of eighty seminarists who were being formed in solid piety and initiated into the Sacred Sciences by a select group of professors.

Lively, expansive, and impressionable, this young seventeen-year old Irishman, whose infectious light-heartedness was at times careless of the formalities, was the life and soul of the group of friends who naturally assembled around him under the attraction of his overflowing good humour and high spirits. His fine intelligence soon revealed a remarkable aptitude for philosphy and theology. What he sought, however, above all in his studies was an inspiration for life. Scripture, theology and the other branches of ecclesiastical learning became the principal nourishment of his piety. He was already developing the spirit of a scholar. A holy Vincentian, Fr. John Gowan, whom he chose as his director, was to have a profound impression on his spiritual life. Humble and austere in himself but impassioned when in his celebrated conferences he spoke of God, of the Passion and Death of Christ, or of the other divine mysteries, he required the same supernatural spirit from his penitents, asking of them a generous acceptance of crosses and humiliations and a fervent devotion to the sufferings of Christ. "Meditate often on the sufferings of Jesus while making the stations of the Cross and you will arrive rapidly at a high degree of perfection." This was his constant advice. It was under his guidance that Dom Marmion formed the resolution to make the stations of the Cross every day, a practice to which he remained faithful to the day of his death.

Under the guidance of such a director Father Marmion made rapid progress in virtue. This is the period of generous —sometimes heroic—personal effort. During an instruction given by a holy priest on fidelity, ten of the seminarists formed the resolution that they would henceforth observe absolutely the rule of silence: "At first" Dom Marmion confesses, "an occasional word would escape me. But I used then to impose a penance on myself and, little by little, I managed to observe the silence absolutely. I think I can say that for five or six years I never failed in this regard."

Apart from his studies he devoted himself in a Sunday school to the instruction of little boys threatened by Protestant propaganda.

During one of the holidays he learned that an old woman, unable to pay her debts, was going to be brought before the courts by a relentless creditor. After an interior struggle lasting the whole night he sacrificed a corresponding sum of money which he had with difficulty saved up for a trip which he had planned. The divine reward was immediate: Father Marmion felt the call to a perfect life developing in his soul.

In 1878 death entered the home. His father died, having had the joy of seeing three of his daughters consecrated to God but without the supreme consolation of seeing his son ascend the steps of the altar as a priest.

This trial was followed by a signal favour in the mystical order which left an ineffaceable impression on his soul. One day as he was about to enter the study hall, he was suddenly overwhelmed " by a light on the infinity of God ". He seemed to be in contact with the inexpressible splendour of God and to catch a glimpse of the immensity of His Being. This only lasted for an instant. He felt immediately a compelling need to prostrate himself in adoration of the divine Majesty. The mystical touches of grace were often to assume in him the character of a sudden dazzling light which finds its fruition in an attitude of faith and adoration.

Rome

His ability, which was well above the average, promised well for the future and Mgr. McCabe sent him to the Irish College at Rome to complete his studies. Fr. Marmion was delighted. " To be in Rome, even apart from studies, is a real education for heart and soul."[3] This does not mean that he despised studies—he showed exceptional brilliance at them

[3] Letter to Dom Idesbald, Louvain, January 12th, 1903.

—but in Rome he found the fulfilment of every spiritual aspiration. " I shall always remember my stay in Rome as one of the happiest periods of my life."[4]

He was particularly impressed by the basilica of St. Peter, the centre point of Catholic unity: *" Hinc unitas."*[5] During his whole life his Christian sense was coupled with a Roman spirit which impelled him to turn instinctively to the Pope as the infallible rule of faith. He visited all the sanctuaries of Rome as a pilgrim, returning with especial enthusiasm to the tomb of the Apostles and to the catacombs, symbolic of a faith professed even to the shedding of blood. For him, Rome meant above all else a living contact with the Church of Christ.

He met many eminent professors at the College of Propaganda, but it was the celebrated Satolli, professor of dogmatic theology, who had the most influence on his intellectual development. It was he who introduced him to the *Summa Theologica* of St. Thomas. To the end of his life Dom Marmion would recall with emotion the admirable teaching of this beloved master. He used to speak in particular of one unforgettable lecture on the beatific vision in which Satolli expounded the supreme joy of which God is the source, in language which was crystal clear but burning with enthusiasm, describing it as the complete satisfaction of the aspirations of the soul in the Absolute Truth and the perfect happiness of the heart in its indefectible union with the Sovereign Absolute Good in the bosom of the Trinity. This divine beatitude was expounded in so impressive a manner that the listeners were at once entranced and captured by the concept and they broke into spontaneous applause when the professor, after giving a resumé of the exposition, closed it with a prayer taken from the psalms: " They shall be inebriated with the plenty of Thy house and thou shalt make them drink of the torrent of Thy pleasure. For with Thee is the fountain of life; and in Thy light we shall see light."[6]

At the end of the scholastic year 1881, Fr. Marmion finished

---

[4] Letter to François X, Maredsous, February 1890.
[5] Inscription on the cupola of St. Peter's.
[6] Ps. xxxv, 9-11.

his studies in Rome. He was first in his class and had won the gold medal.

In June 1881 he received the inestimable grace of Ordination in the eternal city. A month later he returned to Ireland vested with the power of Christ Himself.

Curate in Dundrum

He was appointed curate in the parish of Dundrum, a small village south of Dublin, where he devoted himself to the service of souls in all the varied forms of parochial work.

Professor of Philosophy

A year late Mgr. McCabe appointed him professor of philosophy in the seminary at Clonliffe, which was glad to welcome the former pupil to the staff. It was here that he began to exercise his capacity for clarity of exposition and for penetrating directly to the essentials of a problem which, together with his facility for presenting an effective synthesis of the matter in question, were the characteristic features of his teaching. He remained in intimate contact with souls. An ever increasing number of the seminarists came to him for direction, but he found further scope for his zeal in a very different group disowned by the world: the women's section of Mountjoy Prison where he was chaplain and which housed many political prisoners as well as those convicted of criminal offences. He had also been appointed chaplain to a convent of Redemptoristine nuns. Dom Marmion's natural preference was always for souls consecrated to Christ or for great sinners. It was in teaching and in the direction of souls therefore that he began that apostolic work which was to show such abundant fruit in the spiritual influence of the Prior of Louvain and Abbot of Maredsous.

MONASTIC FORMATION

This full life of study and of apostolic work did not suffice to satisfy all the desires of the soul of Father Marmion. He yearned for a complete dedication to God.

Benedictine Vocation

His first inclination towards a Benedictine vocation had made itself felt on the occasion of a visit to Monte Cassino in 1880 during his stay in Rome, while looking at a fresco in the refectory which represented the Patriarch of the monks of the West: "It was there that I was conscious for the first time of God's call to the monastic life."[7]

On returning to Ireland in May 1881, Father Marmion called at Maredsous to see his friend, Fr. Moreau, who had been a fellow student at Propaganda and had entered the Benedictine novitiate a month before. The abbey, which had been recently founded, made a great impression on this young Irishman: "I arrived at the monastery towards evening. I remember how impressed I was by the peace and silence of the vast cloisters, the chant of the divine office and the sentiment of complete separation from the world which reigned there."[8]

Dom Placide Wolter, who possessed to a rare degree the gift of discerning souls, said to him: "You have a much stronger vocation than your friend."

The hour appointed by God had not yet struck.

In *Presénce de Dom Marmion*,[9] Dom Thibaut has published a very interesting note on the missionary vocation of Dom Marmion. He had planned to serve under Mgr. Salvado, a Spanish Benedictine bishop, founder of New Nursia in Western Australia. He gives some revealing extracts from the two earliest letters of Dom Marmion which we have. They are both addressed to Mgr. Salvado.

Rome, 29 April 1881.

It will doubtless surprise you to learn by this letter that I believe that I have a vocation for your mission in Western Australia.

[7] Letter to the Prior, Dom Robert, Rome, San Anselmo, March 1st, 1912.
[8] Article in the *Belvederian* 1908.
[9] Desclée de Brouwer 1948, pp. 51-58.

I am approaching the end of my theological studies. I was ordained deacon on Holy Saturday and hope to be raised to the priesthood on the Saturday after Pentecost. During the whole period of my studies—that is to say for the last eight years—I have felt a constant attraction for the religious state; I have made repeated efforts, in spite of the vigorous opposition of my family, to realize my desire, but I never succeeded because of the refusal of my bishop—the late Cardinal Cullen—to give his consent.

On the occasion of a visit to Monte Cassino last August I felt all my former desires revive and on my return to Rome my confessor told me that, although he had never advised anyone to become a religious in the course of more than thirty years as confessor to the Irish College, he felt that the signs of my vocation were so evident that he was obliged to give it as his opinion that it was the will of God that I should enter a religious order and, in his judgement, the Benedictine order.

My bishop came to Rome two months later and I opened my heart to him. He, the Most Rev. Dr. McCabe, is a man of great sanctity and, after a day's reflection, he told me that I should first work in his diocese for a time; after which he would place no obstacle in the way of carrying out the will of God; but, as it was a matter of such importance, he thought that it would be more prudent to spend about a year as a secular priest in Dublin and then, if I still felt the call, he promised me his blessing and permission to go. I accepted these conditions and continued my studies as before.

Although I had always felt a great desire for the religious state, I felt at the same time a certain uneasiness or scruple about becoming a Benedictine, in that God had given me an intense eagerness to work for the salvation of souls, and I was always deeply moved when I heard or read about those thousands of human beings for whom Jesus had shed His blood and who die without knowing Him. Therefore, when I happened to read about your mission, I realized that it was to this that I was called, as it would enable me to satisfy my desire to become a religious and at the same time to work for the most neglected souls, and to do so in obedience.

I discussed the matter with François Moreau and my conviction was strengthened. I then consulted my confessor and he told me that he was quite certain that Providence was calling me to this vocation and he gave me permission to write this letter to your Excellency.

Dundrum, June 1882.

I have received your kind letter to which I would have replied before now were it not for the following reason. There has been question recently of assigning to me the duties of private secretary to His Eminence Cardinal McCabe; and while the matter remained open I postponed writing to you from day to day expecting a decision would be reached and that I would be able to inform you of it and have your advice on the line of conduct I should adopt if I were appointed. I had a letter from the Vicar General referring to the appointment, but when the Cardinal came back from Rome my parish priest asked him not to make the change yet and there the matter stands for the moment.

As regards the mission of New Nursia my intentions are as firm as ever and I can speak with the greater conviction as my experience of a year on the secular mission—although it has undoubtedly been very valuable for me—has intensified my desire for the religious life, not with the object of having less to do, but in order to be able to work under obedience and to be separated from the world which unhappily has a great attraction for me.

Providence, which had destined Dom Marmion for a widespread and fruitful apostolate among the clergy, was to keep him for five more years among the priests of the Archdiocese of Dublin.

However, in the depths of his soul the divine call lived on. " In the eyes of the world it seemed that I could not do more good anywhere than where I was; I had all that I needed for my sanctification except one thing—obedience. That is the reason for which I left my country and gave up my liberty and all things. I was a professor; though still young, I had a good position, success, friends. I became a monk in order to obey. God has revealed to me the beauty and the grandeur of obedience."[10]

One letter of Dom Marmion's is especially revealing of his appreciation at this time of the religious life as a consecration to God of a human personality by the total abandonment of its will: " Each religious order has its own beautiful spirit

[10] To his monks.

C

and characteristic virtues which delight the Sacred Heart . . .
if we have not the peculiar spirit and training of the order to
which we belong, we are out of joint in the community and
can never be good religious, nor truly delight the Heart of
Jesus. . . .

"But, you may ask me, 'how am I to gain that spirit, how
am I to know if I really have it?'

"Well, I answer, this is precisely the purpose of the
novitiate; the spirit of the order of Mercy is handed down
from the holy Foundress, through the superiors, and all you
have to do is to leave yourself *absolutely* in their hands
like wax in the hand of one who moulds it, and at the end of
the novitiate the *germs* of that spirit will have been planted
in your heart, to bud forth into perfection later on. This,
with prayer, is the only means of acquiring the spirit of your
state. It is often hard to nature, to be thus cut, and pruned,
but otherwise we can never hope to be pleasing to the Sacred
Heart.

"If I were joining religion to-morrow, I would enter with
the determination of leaving myself *absolutely* in the hands
of my superiors, to let them cut away, *mercilessly,* all the
excrescences of my character so that I might be fit to be presented, as a clean oblation, on the altar of God's love, and
even though nature might repine, I would try to bear all
for the love of Jesus crucified, and I feel sure that if I were
but faithful I would soon acquire the true spirit of my order
and thus 'reap with joy, what I had sown in tears.'[11, 12]

A year later Father Marmion left his beloved Ireland and
sought admission to a foreign monastery. It was on the 21st
of November, 1886, on the feast of the Presentation of Our
Lady. His unexpected departure, of which he had spoken
only to his spiritual director and to his sister Rosie, was a
matter of astonishment and regret for some of his friends;
for others it was the subject of bitter reproaches. "They consider me a kind of apostate for having left the secular clergy.
However, I heard these words: '*Magister adest et vocat te*'.[13]

[11] Ps. cxxv, 6.
[12] Letter to a novice of the Sisters of Mercy, Clonliffe, November 27th, 1885.
[13] John xi, 28.

'The Master is here and bids thee come.' I have obeyed."[14]
There were many who hoped that he would not be able to
bear the cloistered life and foretold an early return. But he
did not come back. When he crossed the threshold of the
monastery it was in the determination to accept the greatest
sacrifices in order to obey God. Father Marmion was formed
in the mould of the saints who do not fall back. "I have
suffered the loss of all things that I may gain Christ."[15]

Novitiate

St. Benedict expects of the postulant a complete "conversion
of life" and the "seeking of God alone," "*Si revera Deum
quaerit.*"[16] The true monk lives alone, apart from the world,
face to face with God. His sole object is to glorify the Lord,
"*Ut in omnibus glorificetur Deus.*"[17] The sole means is
obedience through love. The monastic life, according to the
school of St. Benedict, is "a return to God by the labour of
obedience under the standard of the King of Kings, the Lord
Jesus."[18]
The indispensable condition for this constant search for
God is complete renouncement. Whoever seeks the perfect
life must feel from the very first days how much such a programme requires of him, and Father Marmion experienced
all its severity. The monastic discipline at that time reflected
the vigorous character of the admirable founders of the abbey
of Maredsous, and the poor novice found his thought turning
at times with longing to the peaceful countryside of Ireland.
The novice master did not spare him and the smallness of the
community accentuated the contrasts. Brother Columba
suffered from the loneliness of his life. The Irishman is an
eminently social being. "It is better to be quarrelling than
to be alone," says one of their proverbs. One day, feeling that
he could bear it no longer, the young monk prostrated himself before the tabernacle and in his determination to suffer
all things for Christ he murmured through his tears: "Let me

---

[14] Letter to François X, Maredsous, February 1890.
[15] Phil. iii, 8.   [17] *Rule*, ch. 57.
[16] *Rule*, ch. 58.   [18] Prologue to the *Rule*.

be cut to pieces rather than leave the monastery." Grace had won a decisive victory.

His private notes reveal to us the inner secrets of his soul. Step by step we can follow the constant deepening of his spiritual life.

From the very beginning of his monastic career the adorable figure of Christ stands out in compelling relief in his interior life: "After breakfast, while walking in the garden, I read the eighth chapter of the *Imitation of Christ* and I felt strongly impelled to take Jesus as my one friend. I realized that, in spite of my great weakness and unfaithfulness, Jesus desired to be my friend above all others. The text: 'My delights are to be with the children of men,'[19] gripped me and compelled me irresistibly to respond with all my heart to this desire of Jesus. In the course of this meditation I felt the near presence of Jesus and a great desire to do all things before His eyes."[20]

Two months laters we find this striking note: "On the feast of the Sacred Heart, I felt that we are pleasing to God in proportion as we are conformable to Jesus Christ, especially in His interior dispositions. That is why a childlike confidence in prayer, in spite of our sins, is so pleasing to God. 'I know that You always hear me ',[21] said Jesus. We are the adopted children of God, and we should always, in all simplicity and humility, treat Him in the same way."

We have here in embryo the dominating idea of the spirituality of Dom Marmion. The whole of sanctity consists in our identification with Christ by the grace of adoption. In this note we see a reflection of this central idea.

A "fine passage" from Mgr. Gay gives him "great lights" on the manner of praying in the name of Jesus and he copies it out in full, adding in his notes: "I find Mgr. Gay's chapters on hope and confidence full of light and grace. I hope often to read them.[22]

In the works of Mgr. Gay, who is, on this point, a disciple of the French School, the Person of the Word Incarnate occupies a place of primary importance. It is not surprising, therefore, that Dom Marmion, when asked by one of his

---

[19] Prov. viii, 31.   [21] John xi, 42.
[20] *Private Notes*, April 21st, 1887.   [22] *Private Notes*, September 10th, 1887.

spiritual daughters how she could learn to know Jesus Christ, replied: "Read St. Paul and Mgr. Gay."

These initial graces of the young monk were only the beginnings of a spiritual life which was to bring him to an ever increasing resemblance to Christ· to the point of identification. This was the ideal which he was to put before himself on the day of his solemn profession: "the most perfect imitation possible of Christ."[23]

In his contact with the Benedictine life, Brother Columba discovered the riches of the liturgy. He has not yet attained that lofty personal conception of a soul uniting itself to the canticle of the Word. Liturgical prayer appears to him, in accordance with the classical tradition, as being above all else the expression of the praise of the Church, the Spouse of Christ: "In reciting the Office I derive great help from the thought that I am really an ambassador authorized by the Church to transmit her message to the throne of God many times each day. This message must be delivered in the words and in the way prescribed by the Church."[24]

He was more impressed by the function of praise in the Office than by its impetratory force: "Praise is the highest form of prayer and so pleasing to God that it alone is necessary. It takes the place of all other kinds of prayer."[25]

On the feast of the Most Holy Trinity 1888 he writes: "While reciting the *Gloria Patri* I have great devotion in uniting myself to the adorable Trinity by that eternal hymn of praise which the most Holy Trinity is ever offering to Itself, in infinite love and with the whole heavenly court."[26]

It was not that Brother Columba despised the prayer of petition. One of his favourite attitudes of soul was to intercede "as a member of the Mystical Body of Christ" and, when he ascended the altar he liked to "have in spirit before his eyes the whole world with its miseries, its sufferings and its sins."[27]

Now the praise and the supplication of the Church have

[23] *Private Notes*, February 9th, 1891.
[24] *Private Notes*, May 1st, 1887.
[25] *Private Notes*, between August 17th and September 8th, 1887.
[26] *Private Notes*, Feast of the Trinity 1888.
[27] *Private Notes*, retreat, May 1889.

no value except through Christ. And this was a fact which
could not escape a Dom Marmion. Was it not the fundamental principle of his spiritual life to accomplish all things
in Jesus Christ? "At the time of prayer and especially during the Divine Office I find it a great source of strength to
unite myself with Jesus in His quality of Head of the Church
and advocate with the Father. Jesus exercised His eternal
priesthood in heaven by standing before the throne of the
adorable Trinity and showing His sacred wounds."[28]   And
here we see the dawn already of that great revealing intuition
of the profound sense of the liturgy which is stressed in the
Encyclical of Pius XII: [29] the union of the whole Church with
Christ, the High Priest, in His work of giving praise to the
Father. "Christ is the golden bond of union between all
creation and the adorable Trinity."[30]

While the intellect of the young monk was expanding in
its knowledge of the mystery of Christ and of the richness of
the liturgical life, his will was generously embracing the
practice of all the monastic virtues. He realized that the
Benedictine ideal must from now on be the inspiration of his
sanctity. "God expects of us a perfection, not according to
our own personal concept, but according to the Benedictine
spirit. Failing that, we shall be rejected; and the Code of
this perfection is our Rule."[31]   On the following 13th of
August he writes: "I derive great light from meditating on
the Holy Rule."

There are two characteristic features in his monastic life:
his spirit of detachment and, still more markedly and to a
quite exceptional degree, his practice of religious obedience.
"The words: 'If any man will come after Me let him deny
himself and follow Me,'[32] struck me to-day. *Abnegare*, to
deny oneself, is the opposite of asserting oneself. The more
we efface ourselves, *abneget semetipsum*, the more closely we
follow Jesus."

The familiar texts of the Gospel on renouncement which

[28] *Private Notes*, Feast of the Sacred Heart 1888.
[29] *Mediator Dei et hominum*, November 20th, 1947.
[30] Letter to his sister, a Sister of Mercy, October 17th, 1891.
[31] *Private Notes*, Monday of Quasimodo 1887.
[32] St. Matt. xvi, 24.

he meditated on in the course of his liturgical prayer entered deeply into his soul and became his principle of life: "This morning as we sang the words: '*Vos qui reliquistis omnia et secuti estis me*,' 'You who have left all things and followed me,'[33] I realized that 'leaving' all things has many degrees. There is the material leaving of all things which is very pleasing to God but still very imperfect; the spiritual leaving of all things which is detachment. Finally there is the entire leaving of all things which consists not only in abandoning all that we hold dear but in denying ourselves the joys of memory and imagination in their regard. As spiritual mortification transcends corporal and as spirit transcends materiality, so does this spiritual abandon of all things transcend the merely bodily absence."[34]

But the aspect which impressed him most in this period of monastic initiation was that which had first attracted him to the religious life: the good of obedience: "During Vespers a good thought came to my mind from which I hope to derive great profit: 'Obedience requires us not only to carry out the expressed will of our superiors but also their wishes which we know. Now I know beyond all doubt that it is the formal wish of my Abbot to see us all attain to the highest sanctity possible. Everything else is, in his eyes, secondary, as he has frequently declared. Therefore, the more generous I am in my efforts to attain sanctity, the greater will be my obedience. Thus I can make my life a continuous act of obedience and at the same time a continuous progress in fervour.[35]

On this essential point God gave him clear light: his special grace would always be to go to God by the way of obedience: "I received the grace to understand that for a Benedictine obedience is everything. Mortifications, long prayers, the Mass, may all be impossible or produce very little or even no fruits. Perfect obedience takes the place of everything else. I find great peace in considering things from this point of view."[36]

---

[33] St. Matt. xix, xxix, Mass of a confessor.
[34] *Private Notes*, September 10th, 1887.
[35] *Private Notes*, Pentecost 1888.
[36] *Private Notes*, between September and Christmas 1888.

The Divine lights which he receives are always in the same spirit: "The day after Christmas 1888—The chapter of the Rule: '*Si impossibilia injunguntur*'. 'If you are ordered to do the impossible', seen in the light of the life of Christ, has made a great impression on me. Obedience is the most sublime act of adoration that man can offer to God. This is the keynote of Our Lord's life. All the evils which have afflicted mankind, destroyed the work of God, and peopled hell come from one act of disobedience. All the graces obtained for us by Jesus Christ spring from His obedience. 'In the head of the book it is written of me that I should do Thy will.'[37] O, my God, I wish to accomplish that will and Your law is imprinted in the depth of my heart. The thirty years which Jesus spent in Nazareth are summed up in these words: 'He was subject to them,'[38] and the whole mystery of the Passion is contained in this attitude: 'not as I will but as Thou wilt.'[39] So, every morning, as soon as the bell rings, I shall think of those words of Jesus leaving the bosom of the Father and saying to Him, '*Ecce venio*,' 'Behold, I come.' This shall be the inspiration of my day."[40]

The religious obedience of Dom Marmion found its supernatural motive in the virtue of faith which was the inspiration of his whole life.

"Our Abbot will be to us Jesus Christ in proportion to the faith with which we believe '*eum vices Christi in monasterio gerere*'. How beautiful it would be if we could have Jesus Christ amongst us, as the apostles had Him, to go to Him in our doubts."[41]

Solemn Profession

The soul of Dom Columba was advancing rapidly in perfection. His simple profession marked the first stage. But, in the life of a monk, solemn profession is the supreme, decisive act which pledges his whole existence until death. Dom Marmion appreciated to the full its importance and its

---

[37] Heb. x, 7.
[38] Luke ii, 51.
[39] Matt. xxvi, 39.

[40] *Private Notes*, December 26th, 1888.
[41] *Private Notes*, retreat, May 1891.

grandeur. He made a fervent preparation for this absolute, irrevocable dedication of himself. His private notes give us a precious insight to the secret depths of his soul:

"February 9th, 1891, the eve of my solemn profession. I am filled with gratitude to God for His wonderful goodness to me. On Sunday last, Quinquagesima, I offered Holy Mass in thanksgiving for all the bounty of God, in expiation for my sins and for the intention that my sacrifice might be complete and agreeable to the Lord. I made a good confession after several acts of contrition and I feel now that God will be merciful to me. Great peace."

At this time a single thought dominated his spirit: "Solemn profession is a holocaust, a total gift of oneself to God and the most perfect imitation of Christ. On the day of the Purification in the Temple, Jesus offered himself to His Father without reserve; and, from the time of this, so to speak, official oblation every moment of His life He did 'what pleased His Father,'[42] until, on the Cross, He pronounced His '*Consummatum est.*'

"I have made a firm resolution to imitate this perfect oblation of Jesus by transforming my solemn profession into a holocaust of faith, hope and charity.

"*Faith.* On this, the day of my profession, I surrender into the hands of God all rights over myself in the firm conviction of faith that if, for my part, I give up to Him all that I am and all that I possess, God in return will not fail to inspire my superiors to guide me in all matters by the way which is most in accord with His good pleasure. I feel that this total abandonment is very agreeable to God and gives Him great glory. It is an acknowledgement of His fidelity, and His goodness and constitutes an heroic act of faith.

"*Hope.* I renounce all the goods of this world, declaring solemnly that 'the Lord is the portion of my inheritance,' *Dominus pars hereditatis meae.*[43] This likewise is an heroic act of hope because I look for everything to God, blindly, renouncing the power of directing my own way or choosing my future.

"*Charity.* I sacrifice everything, even my most holy inclina-

[42] John viii, 29.   [43] Ps. xv, 5.

tions, leaving the choice of my occupation entirely to authority in complete disregard of my own tastes. I am solemnly resolved to devote the rest of my life, if obedience requires it, to activities which have no attraction for me or even to those which are entirely repugnant to me."[44]

These are the dispositions of a saint. His own life is the best commentary on this programme; and later on we shall see him giving advice to others in similar circumstances with all the authority of one who speaks from personal experience.

"Enter religion without any projects, without any plan except the one project of belonging entirely to Our Lord and of being, of all the religious, the smallest and the most submissive to those who it may please God to choose to represent Him. You will be a good religious in proportion to your submission and your obedience. Never forget that on your entry into religion and especially on the day of your profession there is an implied contract made between God and you. God undertakes to guide you to perfect love through those who represent Him and He has the power and the wisdom to carry out His part of the contract whoever His representatives may be. For your part, you undertake one thing: to let yourself be guided by your superiors. Sometimes, to test your faith and your fidelity. He will allow your superiors to command something which seems prejudicial to your sanctification but, if you have faith, everything will contribute in the end to your good: *Omnia co-operantur in bonum*.[45, 46]

"Our holy profession contains in embryo the whole of religious sanctity and to achieve perfection in this sublime vocation there is no need to seek beyond this capital grace. A religious profession faithfully observed leads infallibly to sanctity."[47]

This sublime ideal conceived on the day of his profession was not to be for him a mere theoretical concept. It was to be the formula of his life, which he followed in the midst of his daily and varied occupation, united only by the obedience under which they were carried out.

[44] *Private Notes*, February 9th, 1891. [45] Rom. viii, 28.
[46] Letter to P. François de Sales, Louvain, December 27th, 1904.
[47] Ibidem, November 26th, 1905.

Monastic Work

He was at first employed in the Abbatial school as a "surveillant" during the year 1891-92, but his Irish accent, his joviality, and the inevitable misunderstandings which arose on account of his weakness in French were not calculated to assist the maintenance of discipline. This first experience of monastic work was not a success.

On the other hand, in the lessons of philosophy which he gave to the young Desclées he showed exceptional ability. His pupils were loud in their praise of their tutor and soon he was entrusted with the regular courses to the young monks in the Abbey. This decision of his superiors restored him to the sphere of work which was eminently congenial and inaugurated his mission as a teacher of doctrine at which he excelled.

In the early years of a foundation it is inevitable that there should be a certain duplicating of offices: "I began to-day the course of philosophy and this evening I am opening the course of theology. I do not know whether it will be possible for me, with my class in the school and my other occupations, to carry on these courses in a satisfactory way. However, I shall do my best."[48]

There were other activities in store for him. During the eight years preceding his departure for Louvain he carried out, and with unusual perfection, the duties of second master of ceremonies. His taste for the liturgy and his deep understanding of the ceremonials provided ideal nourishment for the contemplative life. Through this sacred symbolism his soul found contact with God. The liturgy was to be at all times one of the chief sources of light for his interior life.

His appointment as Zelator placed him for four years (1895-1899) in the midst of the youth of the monastery who were receiving their formation in the novitiate. Here he came in contact again with the much feared Master of Novices under whose direction he was to work and whose line of action he had to support. The joviality of Dom Columba formed a sharp contrast with the stern asceticism of Dom Benoît. His

[48] Letter to Abbot Hildebrand, Primate of the Order, Maredsous, January 9th, 1891.

infectious gaiety relieved the tension of anxious spirits while his ardent faith helped souls to rise to God. He succeeded excellently in this difficult work and could write to Abbot Hildebrand, who was then in Rome: "Father Master and I live in the closest understanding and there is a remarkable spirit of charity and holy joy in the novitiate."[49]

In June 1895 he revisited Ireland on the occasion of the celebration of the centenary of Maynooth, one of the biggest, if not the biggest, seminary in Christendom. It was in Maynooth that Dom Marmion first met Mgr. Mercier who had been sent to represent the University of Louvain. One can imagine the deep joy which Dom Marmion experienced on returning to his native land in spite of the grief of not finding in the family home some very dear faces which had been removed by death.

In addition to his monastic duties Dom Marmion was called upon in divers circumstances to exercise his zeal outside the monastery in the neightbouring parishes and later in the other towns in the neighbourhood. There was an element of the dramatic in his initiation into pastoral work. A neighbouring parish priest, whose preacher had unexpectedly failed him on the eve of a great feast, came to the Benedictines to ask their help in his difficulty. The superior was very sorry, but he had no one to offer him except a young Irish monk whose French was far from perfect. "I will take him all the same," said the parish priest, and he brought off Dom Columba. Three days later he brought him back to the Abbey saying: "We have never had such a preacher before in my parish." And soon the other parish priests were competing with each other for "the Irish father".

The ministry of Dom Marmion was very varied: he preached to the faithful in the parishes, to young boys and girls in different schools, to workers clubs in the Charleroi district, and gave clergy retreats in Dinant. It was there that he began with his monthly reunions his apostolate among priests which became one of the most characteristic forms of his spiritual influence.

[49] Letter to Abbot Hildebrand, Primate of the Order, Maredsous, 1896 or 1897.

Interior Life

It is in the depths of the soul that one must always seek for the secret of the astonishing fruitfulness of the life of a saint. The great servants of God have to pay with their blood for their power to redeem their fellow men. This is the universal law of redemption. The apostolic influence of Dom Marmion is a striking example of this. During his whole life he was the prey of temptations, hypersensitive, and subject to fits of lassitude, and at times to bouts of depression which were quite disturbing. Grace was not always able to quell the first movements of his nature which was impressionable to a fault. Why should we wonder at this? The weakness of of the saints are a lesson for us and a source of invaluable encouragement. His private notes bear witness with great sincerity to the daily struggles of his nature to rise to the heights of heroic sanctity. A long series of notes mark the stages of his progress.

"Feast of St. Placid, 5 October 1887. Aridity, temptations, weariness."

" 1888. To-day, Monday, I am suffering from nerves and great exhaustion. No sensible devotion, very little light, frequent temptations. *Deo gratias.*"

"Pentecost 1888. Very tired, very much harassed by temptations, but resigned."

"Christmas 1888. In a state of aridity and temptation. *Deo gratias.*"

One could multiply these quotations indefinitely. Dom Marmion, however, by the interior light of the Holy Spirit, was able to understand that these sufferings were for his greater purification.

" 17th February 1895. I have been ill for several months. As well as physical pain, lack of sleep etc., I have been greatly troubled and tormented in soul. At times it seemed to me that I was entirely abandoned by God. But on the feast of St. Scholastica, the anniversary of my profession, the clouds cleared and I realized that these trials and temptations had done a great deal of good to my soul. In particular I have learned what it is to serve God in pure faith. Those who have not passed through such trials cannot know what it is to believe and hope in God in the spirit of faith alone. During meditation those words: 'It is the spirit that quickeneth, the flesh profiteth nothing,'[50] made me see clearly that it is only those acts which proceed from the motive of faith that are supernaturally pleasing to God and that sensible devotion, 'caro,' while helping to produce those acts, is in itself useless, and that those acts which spring solely from sensible devotion have no supernatural value in the eyes of God. Since the tenth of February I am enjoying close union with Jesus in faith though I am still often without the least sensible pleasure. I find little difficulty in keeping myself almost all day long in the presence of Jesus. This in no way interferes with the carrying out of my duties; on the contrary, it is a great help."

Concurrently with these sufferings of struggles and temptation he received many lights,

—lights on the possibility of attaining the highest degree of sanctity by the way of love without being obliged to practise extraordinary austerities which would be beyond his strength.

—lights on the mortification of the senses, on compunction of heart, on the sublimity of his ideal of monastic perfection, on the Eucharist, on devotion to the Blessed Virgin, on the transcendent grandeur of the priestly mission. His contemplative soul was living ever more completely in the supreme light of God.

The end of this first period of his Benedictine life leaves Dom Marmion a fervent monk confirmed in the spirit of renouncement. His vigorous intelligence has made its own those directive principles which were to constitute the main lines of his spiritual doctrine.

As a disciple of St. Paul he had become the passionate lover of Christ.

"I see ever more clearly that Christ is ALL for us." Christ is the centre-point of his doctrine and of his life.

---

[50] John vi, 64.

2. SPIRITUAL DEVELOPMENT

The Louvain period is of capital importance in the evolution of the thought and the spiritual life of Dom Marmion. For ten years the prior of Mont-César was in almost daily contact with the professors and students of the famous University while he himself was engaged in magnificent intellectual activity in connection with his own teaching of the Sacred Sciences. The monastic observance and the silence of the cloister fostered his contemplative life and he exercised a profound influence within the monastery, while the scope of his apostolic zeal was extending ever more widely through his direction of many priests and religious, some of whom had already attained great heights of mysticism. Finally, the graces of enlightenment and of union with God were transforming his interior life. Heroic in his fidelity to obedience and submissive to the least suggestion of the Spirit of Jesus, Dom Columba rapidly ascended the heights of Christian perfection. Louvain was the scene of this period of development.

Prior of Mont-César

Dom Marmion was one of the group of monks who founded Mont-César in Louvain.

Almost from the first days of the Abbey of Maredsous, Dom Gerard Van Caloen, who was later to be the restorer of Benedictine life in Brazil, had propounded the idea of a foundation in Louvain where the monks, while continuing their traditional claustral life, could pursue their studies at the University according to their aptitudes, and provide at the same time for the former pupils of the school at Maredsous who were studying at the University, a hostel where their faith and Christian way of life would be safeguarded in the familiar Benedictine atmosphere.

After a first abortive attempt by Dom Gerard, who fell ill, Dom Robert de Kerchove d'Exaerde was appointed to make preparations for the future foundation. For ten years, single-handed and in face of difficulties which were humanly speaking insurmountable but which he overcame by his confidence in God, he was engaged in buying piece by piece all the land which was to become Mont-César. Dom Robert was a man who produced results. Stern for himself and for others and of extreme tenacity of purpose he was finally to inscribe on his abbatial arms the device of his family: "To endure so that one may last."[1]

On the vigil of the feast of Blessed Ida of Louvain, April 12th, 1899, Dom Robert and his companions in the course of the touching ceremony of farewell received the mandate of the Holy See to set out to make a foundation. They received the blessing of those going on a journey for Christ. They embraced their brethren, and after the solemn chant of *In Viam pacis* they set out, as so many generations of monks had done, to carry further afield the message of Christ.

On the morning of April 13th a little procession of monks led by Dom Robert went right across the town of Louvain. The university city watched them pass, reciting psalms and preceded by the foundation cross. They climbed the slope of Mont-César and at 11 o'clock they entered the temporary chapel to the chant of the *Te Deum* and the *Regina Coeli*. The Benedictine order had given Belgium a new monastery, a centre of prayer and peace, dedicated to the service of God and men. The Abbey of Mont-César was established. It was to develop rapidly into an important centre of spiritual and intellectual life, the influence of which would soon be felt through the entire church. On April 21st, lectures began in this new house of studies, which was made an Abbey on August 6th of the same year, with Dom Robert de Kerchove as first Abbot. He appointed Dom Columba Marmion Prior and prefect of clerics, a double office which he was to occupy until his election as Abbot of Maredsous.

Dom Marmion was at the height of his strength and he devoted himself without reserve to his duties as professor of dogmatic theology and spiritual director.

He had graduated in Rome, had been a brilliant professor of philosophy in Clonliffe and for eight years had devoted himself with scrupulous exactitude to the teaching, first of philosophy and then of theology to his young confrères; all this

[1] "*Endurer pour durer.*"

had served to give him a clearly defined outlook on the world. The fruitful years in Mont-César spent in close contact with the university life enabled him to attain an unrivalled mastery of his subjects. Others may surpass him in the detailed documentation of their learning; but when Dom Columba discusses one of the major theses in which dogma approaches the highest mysteries of God or the fundamental principles regarding the Church of Christ or the spiritual life of the soul, his teaching has a breadth which approaches the infinite. The vast repercussions of his thought, the fruit of long contemplation, throw light on a whole world of secondary conclusions. His trenchant summaries unite with an unusual power of synthesis in one beam of light the diverse aspects of a problem hidden at the first approach in its complexity. The central point stands out in brilliant relief and the whole assembly of connected truths is illuminated by the light of a governing principle which is the key to the whole problem. As a master of synthesis he is unrivalled.

Year by year he covered the whole cycle of classical apologetics and dogmatic theology, penetrating more deeply each time into the traditional foundations of our faith and the principal mysteries of the Christian religion. His treatise *de Verbo Incarnato* is his *chef d'œuvre*; it was the course which he has studied most profoundly together with that of *De Ecclesia,* which was for him a prolongation of the mystery of Christ. The sacraments, Baptism, Penance, and, above all, the Eucharist, occupied his thoughts for a long time. In his course on the elevation of man to the supernatural state he did not lay much stress on the controversies *de auxiliis,* but he analysed scrupulously the fundamental nature of sanctifying grace, that mysterious participation in the divine life which makes us adopted children in Jesus Christ. He dwells on this fundamental point, the very centre-point of all spirituality. It was thus that he elaborated in the course of more than twenty years of deliberate reflection the major theses which were to constitute the basis of *Christ, the Life of the Soul* and his other works, destined to recall modern spirituality to a realization of the most elevated Christian truths and to a new appreciation of the adorable Person of Christ. Having been

D

the matter of his teaching, dogma was now to become the inspiration of his spiritual life.

Here, for example, is his introduction to the study of Grace:

"In the tract on the Incarnation we have seen human nature raised, in Christ, to the dignity of divine Filiation. For this Man, Christ, 'thought it not robbery to be equal to God.'[2] He was truly 'the Son of God'[3] by nature. This partaking of the divine nature[4] was due to Him, the only begotten Son who is in the bosom of the Father.'[5] This elevation to divine Sonship constituted in Christ His uncreated grace, that is to say, the hypostatic union.

"Now God had predestined Christ to become 'the first born among many brethren'[6] so that, He by nature and we by adoption, 'we should be called and should be the sons of God.'[7] In virtue of this grace of adoption 'we enter into fellowship with the Father and with His Son, Jesus Christ.'[8] We thus become 'heirs of God and joint heirs with Christ.'[9] But this elevation of our nature is effected in us by a created grace, the root and source of all our supernatural dignity, and of 'all the gifts coming down from the Father of lights.'[10] Grace is simply this divine gift which raises man to the dignity of the child of God by adoption and which helps him to conform to the grandeur of this condition."

One can recognize here immediately the style of Dom Marmion in which originality is so happily blended with the traditional. The grace of adoption is for him a flowing of the eternal filiation of Jesus into us. For him Christ is the key to everything. His keen mind reduced all problems to the central question of Christ, the Alpha and Omega of the divine plan and the supreme inspiration of his life. "Christ is our Wisdom, and it is by studying Him with reverence and love that we shall at all times find the solution of our theological difficulties."[11]

He follows the same method in the tract on the Church.[12]

[2] Phil. ii, 6.   [5] John i, 18.   [8] I John i, 3; I Cor. i, 9.
[3] John i, 34.   [6] Rom. viii, 29.   [9] Rom. viii, 17.
[4] II Pet. i, 4   [7] I John iii, 1.   [10] Jas. i, 17.
[11] Letter to one of his pupils, Louvain, August 5th, 1902.
[12] Louvain, 1900.

"In approaching any problem it is of sovereign importance to consider everything from above, making a synthetic approach by the light of the superior principle from which it all flows." And he applies this to the mystery of the Church. "She is the Mystical Body of Christ united to Him by a very close bond, filling on earth the rôle of Christ Himself, under the mandate of God, to propose to men with infallible authority the ensemble of revealed truths, and to apply to them all the means of salvation acquired by the merits of Jesus Christ and entrusted to her by her founder."

The Church has its three-fold principle of unity in Christ, Doctor, Priest and King.

Dom Marmion sees all his theological doctrine in the light of the mystery of Christ.

Another duty fell to Dom Marmion in which he felt even more completely at home: the monastic and spiritual formation of the young clerics. While Dom Robert de Kerchove was impressing on his monastery a strict regularity of observance, Dom Marmion breathed into it the warmth and life of a spiritual master.

Twice a week he brought his students together for conferences in which he dealt with the great questions of the spiritual and monastic life. His theological knowledge, his appreciative familiarity with the Scriptures, with St. Paul and St. John, his constant use of liturgical texts which were for himself so fruitful a source of light, and finally, his practical experience and his apostolate among contemplative souls, all these gave to his spontaneous talent the irresistible persuasive force of a vigorous teaching dominated by a passionate, ardent faith in Christ. The expressiveness of his countenance, his occasional use of mimicry, his picturesque and often unexpected flashes of wit all contributed to hold these young men spellbound under the influence of this vigorous personality of a doctor and a saint. His joyous exuberance often puzzled those who judged merely by externals. But when he spoke of Christ and the mysteries of God his whole being was transfigured. His soul was afire with enthusiasm. He found fervent disciples in certain chosen souls like Dom Pie de Hemptinne on whom he stamped the seal of his spirituality.

Dom Marmion commented on the Rule as a spiritual master rather than as a scholar, and the Rule—that complete code of Christian perfection—inspired in him the most varied spiritual teaching to the members of his monastic community. A whole volume of notes taken at these conferences has been preserved. These pages of spirituality, couched in a style which is at times very familiar and at times very elevated, give a foretaste of the doctrinal treasures of *Christ the Ideal of the Monk*. While preserving the spontaneity and simplicity adapted to the intimacy of family intercourse, Dom Columba gives us here all that is best of his religious spirit.

Here again it will suffice to select a few typical extracts: "To become a true monk one must apply oneself to the study of the Holy Rule. Like the Church of which it is a perfect image, the Order of St. Benedict possesses a soul and a body. The soul is the interior spirit; the body the exterior constitution, but they are indivisible. If you destroy one the other disappears."

"The monastery is a society of men campaigning under one Rule and under the leadership of an Abbot, with the object of rendering to God a perfect act of homage: the sacrifice of obedience. Hence the formula of St. Benedict: 'Prefer nothing to the divine Office.' *Nihil operi Dei praeponatur.*[13]

"As regards other works, the monk undertakes them only in virtue of obedience and to pay homage to God. Not that all works are to be regarded as on the same plane, but for a monk no work has any real value except in so far as it is an expression of his obedience, his homage, and his sacrifice. The monk is an ideal Christian, for the monastic order is simply Christianity in its perfection."[14]

It is not difficult to appreciate the tone of these extracts, and to imagine the value of the practical application to which the Prior of Mont-César was able to put them in all the varied circumstances of the life of a great Abbey in the process of formation.

The little foundation group of monks was not yet a large

[13] *Rule*, ch. 43.
[14] Monastic conferences at Louvain, between 1899 and 1909.

community, but it was necessary to lay a solid foundation for the future.

As an experienced master of the spiritual life, Dom Marmion in the course of his weekly conferences stressed the primary importance of the interior life and the faithful practice of the monastic virtues, not ostentatiously or in a pharisaical spirit, but for love, in the spirit of liberty of true children of God.

"The object of the monastic life is to arrive at the perfection of love so that it becomes the active principle of all the virtues. Love is at once a means and an end. Our eternal happiness will depend on our degree of love at the hour of death. We must strive therefore to increase this love, not only for the greater glory of God, but for our own personal advantage. St. Paul tells us that the most heroic actions without charity are of no value."[15] The only thing that counts in the eyes of God is charity. He who possesses love possesses all the other virtues which spring from it.

It is in this sense that we must understand the words of St. Augustine: "Love and do what you like." Dom Columba adds wisely: "True love consists in doing the will of Him who loves us. If we really love Our Lord we shall practise all the virtues enumerated by St. Paul in his definition of charity: "Charity is patient, is kind, thinketh no evil, etc." Love of God is therefore the end and the means of all spiritual progress, but it must never be separated from a reverential and affectionate fear of God which will be our safeguard against pride and every kind of concupiscence. He who possesses the true love of God, says St. Paul, is guided by the Holy Spirit to accomplish all that God wills.

The fundamental disposition of a monk must be one of perfect docility to the Spirit of love. "This submissiveness marks the essential difference between souls. One sees sometimes religious whose observance is very exact and who make no spiritual progress; later one discovers the reason: a lack of suppleness of soul in regard to obedience or fraternal charity. The submissive souls, on the other hand, are very dear to the heart of God. If at times they are betrayed into exterior

[15] I Cor. xiii, 2.

faults, God overlooks them and raises them up lovingly because their perfect docility compels His merciful love."[16]

This perfection is not a mere theory. The monk finds his true model in Christ. "A spiritual life which does not depend entirely on Christ is false, empty, absolutely useless. 'Without me you can do nothing.'"[17] At all times Dom Marmion directs souls towards Christ.

To this teaching the Prior of Mont-César added the irresistible force of example.

The Prior holds an important place in the organization of a Benedictine abbey, below the Abbot, who appoints and dismisses him at will. An intermediate and difficult position, second to the Abbot but not a second Abbot. "There are some in fact", St. Benedict remarks, "who, swollen with an evil spirit of pride, imagine themselves second Abbots: they assume uncontrolled authority, encourage scandals and cause dissensions in the community. From this there arises jealousies, conflicts, detractions, rivalities, factions and the greatest evils. If the Abbot and the Prior are opposed to each other, those who live under their guidance take sides for one or the other and risk the loss of their souls."[18]

In his conception of the monastic community St. Benedict insists on the absolute primacy of the Abbot as the source and safeguard of unity. For the preservation of peace and charity the government of the monastery must depend entirely on the Abbot.[19] And the holy patriarch prudently counsels the Prior to do nothing against the will of the Abbot, *Nihil contra abbatis voluntatem aut ordinationem faciens.*[20] The Prior must at the same time command and obey. It is a difficult position which calls for a great deal of tact, prudence, charity, and humility.

At first sight the contrast between Dom Robert de Kerchove and Dom Columba Marmion was striking even in the physical order. The Abbot of Mont-César was an ascetic, emaciated angular man, clear-cut and firm in his attitudes and requiring

---

[16] Monastic conferences, Louvain, 1899-1909.
[17] John xv, 5.   [19] *Rule*, ch. 65.
[18] *Rule*, ch. 65.   [20] *Rule*, ch. 65.

a meticulous observance of the Rule and of his wishes. For the rest, one of the great race of monks whose work has the durability of granite. Dom Marmion was a man of noble corpulence, jovial and bantering, permitting himself at times a full-blooded Irish joke; but as soon as the hour of prayer sounded he could be seen to fall into deep recollection. His contemplative soul was immediately carried away with Christ to the bosom of the Father.[21]

There were times, it must be admitted, when the obedience of the Prior of Mont-César had to attain heroic heights to remain faithful. He never failed, submitting, effacing himself, not only without a word of recrimination, but without even letting anyone suspect the measure of the sacrifice required of him, acting as he did in a spirit of faith which enabled him to see at all times Christ in the person of his Abbot.

After one of these severe trials he was able to write in all honesty: "You will be glad to know that Our Lord has given me a very great grace—the greatest, I think, of my whole life —for in spite of a severe interior struggle He has given me the grace, not only to submit myself unreservedly to Father Abbot but also to continue to give him all my confidence and all my affection and to resolve to remain here, if such be His holy will when the time comes to make the choice. While at prayer I realized that everything consists in this: to receive Christ in whatever form He may be pleased to present Himself; be it as a gardener, as a pilgrim, as a sympathetic character or the reverse; to receive Him, not half-heartedly or coldly, but whole-heartedly, loyally, frankly, and the more He may strike us, the more we should bow our heads. I cannot express to you the delicious peace and perfect liberty of heart which I enjoy."[22]

The Prior of Mont-César admired the virtue, the strength of character and the administrative capacity of his Abbot: he venerated him as a saint. All these sufferings, inevitable in community life, served to purify the ardent and impulsive spirit of Dom Marmion. The austere monastic discipline of

[21] St. John, i, 18.
[22] Letter, Louvain, April 1st, 1902.

Louvain was a salutary check on his easy-going nature and kept him up to his heroic dedication to God. The example of his fidelity lent immense weight to his teaching. In his complete devotion to the community he accepted unquestioningly his full share of the drudgery of all kinds which this period of foundation imposed.

In 1923, immediately after the death of Dom Columba, Dom Robert de Kerchove, speaking to the nuns of Maredret, bore testimony to this admirable fidelity: "I had him as my Prior for ten years and I was always edified by his charity and devotion to the service of the monastery. As for his obedience, I can affirm that I have never had a more obedient monk." And in February 1942, when he was dying, this venerable monk, then ninety years of age, said to Dom Thibaut: "What an extraordinary man he was! I must have made him suffer, but I have never met a more obedient religious."[23]

In view of such abnegation can we wonder at the great spiritual fruits of this daily joyous devotedness: "Here all goes well, thanks be to God," Dom Marmion writes to the Abbot of Erdington, "God blesses us, not with temporal goods, but with great peace and a holy union in charity. As we seek this first, all the rest will be added unto us.[24] Our studies are progressing in all branches. There is great enthusiasm and the results are very satisfactory."[25]

Side by side with Dom Robert and in close union with him, the Prior led souls on to God and contributed with all his energy to the establishment of the abbey in unity and peace.

Relations with the outside world

A Benedictine abbey in the centre of a great University town is very different from a Chartreuse in the wilderness. As soon as they had arrived in Louvain, the sons of St. Benedict found themselves involved in the intellectual life of the

---

[23] *Présence de Dom Marmion*, p. 69.
[24] Matt. vi, 33.
[25] Letter to the Abbot of Erdington, Louvain, January 2nd, 1900.

famous university. "The Rector has come to invite the professors to take part in the theological and philosophical discussions. This is not entirely to my taste; but we cannot refuse, as we are, with the Jesuits and the Dominicans, the three houses of study and we must accept the responsibilities of our position."[26]

Dom Marmion, now in his full maturity, and deeply versed in theology, was in particular demand. He had to attend repeatedly at the university to assist at the defence of theses, or to propose objections on the occasion of academic disputations. A considerable book of notes in his own handwriting bears witness to the care with which he prepared these contributions which were at once learned and humorous, and delighted the select audiences which assembled on these occasions in the Aula Maxima of the University.

It was not long before bonds of friendship were established between the professors and students of the different faculties and the abbey of Mont-César, where they were received for retreats, for days of recollection, or as simple visitors, in accordance with the best tradition of Benedictine hospitality. They soon learned to feel at home in this house of prayer and peace. There was a constant coming and going between the Abbey and the University. Both professors and students were quick to discover the value of the Prior of Mont-César as a spiritual guide. Many priests came to put themselves under his direction. Every Friday one might see little groups of priests climbing the slope leading up to the Abbey on their way to Dom Marmion's cell, where they found a ready source of light and peace.

Among the many distinguished people who used to come to consult the Prior of Mont-César the most distinguished was Mgr. Mercier, who had chosen Dom Columba as his confessor. He consulted him regularly and was at all times a constant visitor and a faithful friend to Mont-César. It was there that he received formal notification of his elevation to the cardinalate; there also that he composed in 1914 his famous letter: "Patriotism and endurance," which achieved world-wide fame.

[26] Letter to Dom Bede, Louvain, August 1899.

When Mgr. Mercier was appointed Archbishop of Malines, Dom Marmion felt the separation keenly: " I have lost a very dear friend in Mgr. Mercier. For many years we have been so intimate that we have had practically no secrets between us. Now his high position creates a gulf which all his condescension cannot bridge. . . . He is a holy man who seeks only God and His glory. He will do great things for souls."[27]

In fact Providence was to bring them together frequently and Dom Columba always professed great veneration for his illustrious friend: " He is a real saint."[28]

But it was among contemplatives that the genius of Dom Marmion appeared to the best advantage. Talking to them intimately he was able to speak without restraint, and he carried away the souls of his listeners to the highest summits of the mystical life, "to the bosom of the Father." [29]

The Carmelites of Louvain were the first to submit themselves to his spiritual direction. He undertook their guidance with paternal kindness: " I accept the responsibility of your direction as an order coming from Him to whom I owe all things, and I shall try by my poor prayers and my ministry to help you to attain to that sublime perfection to which your heavenly Spouse is calling you. . . . My desire is that Jesus be the sole director of the Carmel of Louvain. It is He who has ransomed you with His Precious Blood. It is to Him and to Him alone that you belong. It is for Him to sanctify you, and if He designs to make use of me in this work which is so important for His glory, it will be on the condition that I always act in dependence on His Spirit, and that I seek in His Sacred Heart the light to understand His designs for each individual soul."[30]

Every week the Prior of Mont-César went faithfully to the Carmelite convent as ordinary confessor, and gave the nuns spiritual conferences which were carefully noted down. He

[27] Letter to Dom Robert, Louvain, April 30th, 1906.
[28] Letter to a nun of the Dames Anglaises de Bruges, Maredsous, March 14th, 1914.
[29] John i, 18.
[30] Letter to the Prioress of the Carmel of Louvain, Maredsous, February 20th, 1899.

paid weekly visits also to the American college to hear the confessions of the students.

Every month, in addition to his conferences to the University College of the Holy Ghost of which Mgr. Ladeuze was president, he went to Brussels to speak to the English colony there. During the last two years of his life at Louvain he took charge, at the request of Cardinal Mercier, of the days of recollection for the parochial and teaching clergy in the capital.

Other communities in ever-increasing numbers asked for the privilege of his guidance: he was called to religious houses in Louvain, Liège, Bruges, Jupille, Lede, Kocekelberg, and many other towns in Belgium, Ireland and England: he gave retreats to the communities at Douai, Ampleforth, Ramsgate, Erdington, Stanbrook and Princethorpe. In spite of the overwork and exhaustion incident to the closing months of the scholastic year it was his custom to devote the summer months to this ministry. "I am leaving for England at the end of next month to give retreats. It is my way of taking a rest. I would not care for holidays which served no useful purpose."[31] Added to all this we have the various unforeseen events and extraordinary circumstances inevitable in a widespread and varied apostolic activity, from which he acquired a comprehensive understanding of souls and by which his own soul was marvellously enriched.

In spite of himself, the Prior of Mont-César was drawn into a whole series of apostolic engagements which left him less and less breathing space. It was found necessary to relieve him of some of his courses of theology. He accepted this decision with a certain regret. "I must confess that it is a sacrifice to have to give them up just when I was beginning to perceive the synthesis of all these splendid problems."[32]

The force of his personality was making itself felt outside the monastery. Cardinal Mercier sent frequently for his confessor and friend. He brought him with him to Maria Laach (October 1907), to Paray le Monial (March 1909), to Rome (February 1912). His major superiors made the fullest

[31] Letter to Dom Thibaut, Louvain, July 24th, 1906.
[32] Ibidem, March 10th, 1904.

use of him for the good of the Order, and in July 1909 he assisted at the chapter-general in Beuron. His relations with the outside world were ever increasing. He was in demand on all sides. His Abbot had to defend him from those who were importuning his services and to protect him also from himself. There was a danger that his apostolic zeal and the combination of monk and missionary in his character might lead him to undertake too much activity, but his spirit of perfect submission was an effective protection against this tendency: "I feel more and more the need to give myself to the service of souls, but at the same time Jesus makes it clear to me that, as a monk, all my activity must be ruled and inspired by Him through obedience."[33]

He was not dazzled by his success: "I feel that there is such a distance between my preaching and my practice that I really tremble lest I become like a signpost pointing the way for others and remaining stationary myself."[34]

In spite of everything, as the years went by, his work increased: "I am on the commission of vigilance for this diocese, which means work, work."[35]

The same complaint reappears frequently in his letters: "You have no idea how my time is eaten up. I say 'eaten', because every morning I place myself on the paten with the host which is to become Jesus Christ. And just as He is there to be eaten by all sorts of persons—*sumunt boni, sumunt mali, sorte tamen inaequali*—so I am eaten all day long. May our beloved Saviour be glorified by my destruction as He is by His own immolation."[36]

It is difficult to understand how one man could cope with so many varied activities. There were his regular courses in theology and Scripture, which required long hours of preparation; discussions on the current theological problems with the professors and students of the University, consultations, both written and oral, with different religious authorities who

---

[33] Letter to the Abbess of Maredret, February 23rd, 1903.
[34] Letter to a nun of the Dames Anglaises at Bruges, Louvain, January 8th, 1908.
[35] Ibidem.
[36] Letter to Sister Cecilia of Maredret, Louvain, January 19th, 1905.

wished to have the support of his doctrinal competence in this era of the modernist crisis, or to take advantage of his exceptional knowledge of the protestant sects.

His apostolic zeal and his experience of the spiritual life made him much sought after as a preacher of retreats and as a spiritual director. These labours, which were very exhausting in themselves and which were the outcome of his special personal qualities, were in addition to his daily round of absorbing work, the constant demands of social life which his position as a Prior involved him in, and an ever-growing correspondence, not to mention the flow of visitors and the thousand and one unexpected interruptions of the daily life of a monastery situated in the middle of a city.

In spite of all this Dom Marmion was strictly faithful to all the monastic observances and to all the regular exercises of the house, and in particular to the Office in choir where he was the first to arrive, and where he liked to prolong the liturgical prayer by private converse with God. He was always in the midst of everything, taking his share of the work and other duties of the common life as well as the recreations, where his animation and good humour would drive away the cares of his confrères with some unexpected joke. He was sometimes perhaps a little unconventional, but he could also quite naturally rise swiftly to the supernatural plane with all the spontaneity of a man whose whole heart was given to Christ.

Here lies the secret of this extraordinary life. The Prior of Mont-César harboured the soul of a saint.

Tendency towards identification with Christ

The prodigious activity of the Prior of Mont-César is at first sight bewildering and one is tempted to wonder whether it was really possible for him to be faithful to his monastic vocation. But we have the testimony of history that for many centuries before the foundation of the mendicant Orders and the modern Congregations—and even since then—monasticism has provided innumerable apostles to the Church according to the needs of the times. It would be a grave underestimation of the great Benedictine ideal, one of the highest and most liberal forms of christianity, to wish to restrict its formula of realization strictly according to the more modern classifications of activity and contemplation. According to the school of St. Benedict, and according to the Gospel, Christian perfection is compatible with every form of human activity. It consists essentially, not in this or that form of regular observance, but above all in the direction of one's whole existence towards the search for God, in a life of intense faith expressing itself under the impulse of charity and according to the needs of the Mystical Body, in the most varied forms of apostolic activity.

It is this broad concept of the Benedictine ideal which explains the life of the Prior of Mont-César, which was at the same time deeply contemplative and extremely active. Dom Marmion with his individual temperament appears to us as the incarnation of Irish monasticism with its missionary vocation, ready to devote itself in distant lands for the conquest of souls in the service of the Church of Christ.

As he advanced in years his soul achieved in ever-increasing measure that superior harmony in which the interior life and an overflowing activity were happily united in the same forceful personality. It is manifest in him everywhere: in the solitude and silence of the cloister, where his soul was bathed in the plenitude of God, as well as in the busy cities of Brussels and London, or in his journeys across Germany or Italy wherever the duties of his position led him. Through it all his truly monastic soul was seeking God and his apostolic heart maintained its longing for Christ. The crowd or the solitude made little difference to him; the one object of his interior life was Christ.

In this Louvain period we can see him tending more and more to union with the Soul of the Word Incarnate in sentiments of praise and adoration. He was achieving a simplification of his interior life. Soon he was to look for only one thing: identification with Jesus in His intimacy with the Father.

When he arrived in Louvain his spiritual life was already centred in Christ. This was the fundamental tendency of his soul, his particular grace amounting to a supernatural gift, which was to make him the doctor and tireless preacher of the infinite riches of Christ. His contact with the University, far from inclining his contemplative soul towards an arid intellectualism, drew him ever closer to the Unique Source of life—Christ Jesus. " To-day the 29th of September, 1899, I received a special grace. I realized that all my perfection must consist in intimate union with Jesus Christ as Son of God and Saviour of mankind. I realized this clearly after my Mass. And thus my thanksgiving consists of making my own the acts of Jesus in regard to His Father and in regard to my soul and those of others."[37]

A new scholastic year was beginning. He recommenced his intellectual work joyously, but the centre point of his life was the liturgy which united him to all the mysteries of Christ. The climax was the feast of Easter. In the paschal mystery Dom Marmion saw clearly the double aspect of death and life which was the inspiration of his spiritual doctrine: the mystery of death to sin and life in God with Jesus. " '*Quod autem vivit, vivit Deo,*'[38] ' In that He liveth He liveth unto God.' I have felt the intensity of this life of Jesus *all for God.* (the italics are his.) To unite our life with this life is the highest form of perfection. ' Without Him we can do nothing.'[39] And it is just to communicate this life to us that He has come. ' As the Father hath life in Himself, so He hath given to the Son also have life in Himself.'[40] ' I am come that they may have life and may have it more abundantly.'[41] I have felt more and more keenly the desire to associate myself with this divine life so that Jesus might be glorified in me . . . I have made the resolution to try to unite my poor life to this intense divine life."[42]

With the passage of the weeks and months in the midst of his many exhausting occupations his soul was plunged ever more deeply in Christ, to the point of losing itself in Him in the unity of the same love of the Father. " Our Lord is inviting

[37] *Private Notes*, September 29th, 1899.
[38] Rom. vi, 10.   [40] John v, 26.
[39] John xv, 5.   [41] John x, 10.
[42] *Private Notes*, April 18th, 1900, Easter Tuesday.

me to become identified with Him. . . . He is urging me to
make acts of love of the Father in union with Him, to abandon
myself entirely to Him, to love my neighbour as He has loved
him. It is this last point which has appealed to me especially
for some time. I am conscious of a great increase of love for
the Church, the Spouse of Christ. I have formed the habit of
seeing Jesus Christ in my neighbour and I am filled with a
great spirit of charity towards everyone. I can see very clearly
that true charity embraces all the virtues and requires a constant renouncement. As a practice of the interior life I feel
an ever-growing urge to *lose myself in Jesus Christ* that He
may deign to accept me and bear me to the Father."[43] These
confidences to the Abbot Primate reveal to us the habitual
state of his interior life and its dominant characteristic:
identification with Christ. His soul tasted freely of these
divine contacts and his ministry constantly extended his personal experience, but all these lights, acquired and infused,
and all these graces of union were concentrated on the one
central truth which dominated his outlook. For him, Christ
is not merely one of the elements of our perfection. He is the
all in our spiritual life. Dom Marmion returns constantly to
a text of St. Paul which had enlightened him on this capital
point, and where he found a formula to express the divine
plan. "*Christus factus nobis sapientia a Deo et justitia et
sanctificatio et redemptio*," "Christ Jesus, who of God is made
unto us wisdom and justice and sanctification and redemption."[44] The soul of Dom Marmion found its full expression
in this atmosphere of Christo-centrism. "If I am asked in
what the spiritual life consists, my reply is: Christ."[45]

His private notes, his correspondence, his retreats, his conferences to priests and his day-to-day advice to the monks of
Mont-César mark the ascending curve of this transformation
into Christ. "I am very much united to Our Lord, more, I
think, than ever before in my life . . . I feel more and more
urged to lose myself, to hide myself in Christ. '*Vivens Deo*

[43] Letter to Abbot Hildebrand, Primate of the Order, Louvain, June 1st,
1901.
[44] I Cor. i, 30.
[45] Letter undated, quoted in *Union à Dieu*, p. 53, by Dom Thibaut.

in Christo Jesu.'[46] He is becoming, as it were, the eye of my soul. My will is becoming identified with His. I feel urged to desire nothing outside of Him so that I may remain in Him. So much for my state of soul."[47]

He was reading at this period the *Treatise on the Love of God* of St. Francis de Sales, who had become his favourite spiritual author. He adopted his doctrine of abandonment and holy indifference but integrated it in his own personal system, wishing to live it in Christ. " My interior life is becoming ever more simple—tending to unite my will to that of the Eternal Father through Jesus Christ. I feel called to suppress every desire except that of accomplishing the *known will* of God with all the energy of my soul; and, in order to please God, of abandoning myself without plan or desire to His Wisdom and Goodness."[48]

Some months later he summed up his attitude: "It all amounts to this—loving Jesus Christ."[49]

This profound union with Jesus put his soul in communion with all the members of the mystical body of Christ. His life expanded under the vast horizons of the unity of the Church and assumed an infinite extension.

It was in this constant union with Christ that Dom Marmion found the motive force for his apostolic zeal, his fraternal charity, his spirit of prayer, his practice of the virtues and, indeed, for all his activity, interior and exterior. It was in seeking this identification with Jesus that he found his supreme ideal of sanctity: to live with Him " in the bosom of the Father."[50] This Joannine formula, which expresses this profound mystery of the Word hidden in the bosom of the Father, was to become henceforth the motif of his personal life of union with God. The echo which this formula awoke in those privileged souls who were under his direction gave him daily confirmation of its inexhaustible depths. The private notes of the last years at Louvain show us to what a degree it had become his personal ideal. The grace of adop-

[46] Rom. vi, 2.
[47] Letter to the Abbess of Maredret, Louvain, October 28th, 1902.
[48] Letter to Abbot Hildebrand, Louvain, December 26th, 1902.
[49] Letter to the Abbess of Maredret, Louvain, April 9th, 1903.
[50] John i, 18.

E

tion identified him with the intimate life of the Son in the bosom of the Father.

"*In sinu*: this is the final intimacy of affection which supposes perfect love, confidence, and union of will. So it was with St. John at the Last Supper. United with Jesus, we are *in sinu Patris*. This is the life of pure love which presumes the effort to do always what is most agreeable to the Father. 'He hath not left me alone, for I do always the things that please Him.'[51] Our weakness and our wretchedness do not prevent us from being *in sinu Patris* because it is the bosom of infinite Love and infinite Mercy. All this supposes a profound abasement and distrust of ourselves, all the greater because we are so close to this infinite sanctity. It supposes also that we put our trust in Jesus '*Who of God is made unto us wisdom and justice and sanctification and redemption.*'[52]

"All that we do in the bosom of the Father in a filial spirit is of immense value. But this state supposes the absence of all deliberate fault and complete readiness to follow the inspirations of the Holy Spirit. For Jesus has taken on Himself 'our infirmities and our miseries', but He cannot accept the least deliberate sin: 'Which of you shall convince me of sin?'[53] It is in this sanctuary that graces are lavished on us even to the point of the gift of contemplation."[54]

In this passage, in which he rises to sublime heights, Dom Marmion reveals to us the supreme secret of his soul and of his personal intimacy with God. In all the great mystics we find the horizons of their spiritual life extending sooner or later towards the adorable Trinity. With Dom Marmion it was Christ who brought him to the Word and the Word bore him away to the bosom of the Father. The operation of his soul did not lead him, as in the case of Elizabeth of the Holy Trinity, to a direct contemplation of the three divine Persons. Modelling himself on Christ in His essential state, Dom Marmion's approach to the Father was in accordance with the attitude of the soul of the Son.

A very precious document which has been preserved is an act of consecration to the Holy Trinity which he composed

[51] John viii, 29.   [53] John viii, 46.
[52] I Cor. i, 30.   [54] *Private Notes*, April 22nd, 1906.

himself in collaboration with the Carmel of Louvain and where we find reproduced the profound rhythm of his interior life.

"O Eternal Father, prostrate in humble adoration at your feet we consecrate our whole being to the glory of Your Son, Jesus, the Word Incarnate. You have constituted Him the King of our souls; make subject to Him our souls, our hearts, our bodies, and let nothing in us operate except by His orders and His inspiration. United to Him may we be borne to Thy bosom and consummated in the unity of Thy love.

"O Jesus, unite us to Thee in Thy most holy life which is consecrated to the Father and to souls.

"Be our wisdom, our justice, our justification, our redemption, our All. Sanctify us in truth. O Holy Spirit, Love of the Father and the Son, take up Thy abode as a furnace of love in the centre of our hearts and bear upwards like eager flames our thoughts, our affections, and our actions to the bosom of the Father.

"May our whole life be a Gloria Patri et Filio et Spiritui Sancto.

"O Mary, Mother of Christ, Mother of fair love, form us in the image of the heart of your Son."

The whole mystical spirit of Dom Marmion is expressed in this prayer.

3. FINAL TRANSFORMATION INTO CHRIST

In 1903, Dom Columba fixed his stability at Mont-César. It seemed that he was attached to the abbey of Louvain for life. Providence, however, had arranged otherwise.

Leo XIII had appointed Dom Hildebrand de Hemptinne the Abbot of Maredsous, primate of the Benedictine Order. Experience made it clear to Dom Hildebrand that he could not combine for long the important duties of Primate, which required long periods in Rome, with the effective government of his abbey. A successor had to be found and the name of Dom Columba had already been freely mentioned. The possibility had even come to the ears of Dom Columba himself. His first reaction was to recoil from the responsibility. " I honestly believe that I am incapable of it. That is why I am far from desiring it or seeking it."[1] As the hour of the election approached he abandoned himself entirely to the will of God: " I am in perfect peace, for my sole desire is that the will of God be accomplished, and I am sincerely convinced for many reasons that the position is far beyond my capacity."[2] " Pray hard for me in these days so that whatever may happen I may accept it in the way that Our Lord would wish me to accept it."[3]

When the result of the election reached Mont-César on September 28th, 1909 Dom Marmion was at first overwhelmed. But grace triumphed: " A great struggle and great temptations of discouragement and despair during last night. After celebrating the Mass of St. Michael great peace and confidence."[4] The same day Dom Marmion left for Maredsous where he received the promise of obedience from his monks.

Abbot of Maredsous

Every change of government brings its own special grace. Dom Placide Wolter gave the great Beuron spirit of religion and established the scrupulous fidelity to monastic observances in Maredsous. The brothers Wolter laid the foundations, material and spiritual, of the monastery. Dom Hildebrand de Hemptinne, who was the next in succession, gave a great impulse of expansion to the abbey: it was he who started the School of Arts, founded Mont-César, restored Benedictine life in Brazil, and became the Abbot Primate of the whole Benedictine Order. Dom Columba, for his part, was the doctor and master of the spiritual life.

[1] Letter to the Abbess of Maredret, Louvain, May 12th, 1905.
[2] Letter to a nun of the Dames Anglaises of Bruges, Ramsgate, September 7th, 1909.
[3] Letter to Mother Garnier, foundress of Tyburn, Malines, September 20th, 1909.
[4] *Private Notes*, September 29th, 1909.

Conscious of his rôle as representative of Christ, he made the well-known formula of St. Benedict the guiding principle of his government: *"Abbas vices Christi,"* "The Abbot takes the place of Christ in the monastery."[5]

This principle directed every aspect of his abbatial functions: he was the pastor and father of souls, the doctor and the pontiff. *In Christ, the Ideal of the Monk*, Dom Marmion describes this triple rôle of the Abbot. The views which he expresses here, drawn from his personal experience, bring out the characteristic traits of his own ideals.

Like Christ, the Abbot is the Father of the souls in his monastery. His mission as pastor is to lead them to God. The whole conduct of the monastery must be directed towards this end. The temporal and spiritual are indissolubly united in a well-organized monastery. Dom Marmion found himself at the head of a prosperous monastery with a diversity of activities: a hundred monks, a school, a school of arts, as well as various literary and scientific undertakings which provided scope for the intellectual activity of the community and extended far and wide the fame of Benedictine learning and spirituality. In fact it was a complete little city that he had to govern. It must be admitted that Dom Marmion had not himself any gift for administration, but he was able to surround himself with capable officials and under his rule the abbey enjoyed continuous prosperity.

He exercised an understanding and beneficent guidance over the varied and fruitful apostolic activities of his monastery, maintaining and improving the existing works and encouraging initiative and every form of zeal compatible with the monastic ideal in the service of the neighbouring parishes, the diocese, and the whole Church. He sent monks to Rome to staff the Greek College of St. Athanasius, to study at the international College of San Anselmo, to take part in the pontifical work of the revision of the Vulgate. Further afield he participated in the missionary activity of the Church in the evangelization of the Congo. But it was in the government of souls that he showed himself

---

[5] *Rule*, ch. 2.

a master, inspiring all round him a vigorous impulse towards sanctity.

The newly elected Abbot entered on his duties full of good will, full of confidence in divine grace, and eager to devote himself to the service of his brethren. He had chosen as the device of his abbatiate the maxim of St. Benedict: *"Magis prodesse quam praeesse."* "To be of service rather than to command." He took occasion later on to give his monks the following vivid commentary on it: "The Abbot must try to do good rather than to control. There are some people who always want to take charge of everything: *praeesse magis quam prodesse.* We have an Abbot because there must be someone at the head of things, but he must do all that he can to be of service: *prodesse.* Our holy Father goes even further than that: *Studeat plus amari quam timeri*: "Let him seek to be loved rather than feared." His government must be paternal so that his monks may work for love rather than from fear. I pray constantly for each one of you and offer my Mass frequently for you. My great desire is to do you good, my great pleasure is to give you pleasure. When I have to refuse anything to anyone it causes me more pain than it does to the one who is refused. When God imposes a charge on someone, say St. Bernardine of Siena, He owes it to Himself to give him the light and graces necessary to his position. There are abbots who are always anxious: *qui nunquam requiescunt.* For my part I detest watching people: I trust you. It is for you to respond to my confidence by loyalty. My dear sons, I want to develop love in this abbey rather than fear. I often ask myself how I could give pleasure to so and so. I want to arrive at ' being loved rather than feared.' *Plus amari quam timeri,* not just for the pleasure of being loved, that would be childishness, but so that the service of the monks may be a service of love."[6]

As soon as he arrived at Maredsous, his great goodness, his supernatural spirit, and the splendour of his doctrine won all hearts. He experienced those consolations which superiors in the religious life generally experience on their entry into

[6] Conference, Maredsous, August 20th, 1916.

office: "My monks are wonderfully docile and do their best
to help and support me."[7] But it was no easy task to rule
beings endowed with free will, and less than a year after his
election we find Dom Colomba feeling already the weight of
his burden . "I have suffered a great deal since I became
Abbot, but I have suffered in silence. More than once when
I was obliged, for reasons which I could not reveal, to remove
one of my monks from his office, I was challenged to explain
the reasons for my action, which I could not do without revealing the secrets of another's soul. The burden and the
responsibilty are so great that if I followed my own inclination,
I would ask the Holy Father to relieve me of them. Not a day
passes without trials of this kind. I have had some very severe
ones in the last few days. I have had to keep them to myself
and when, in addition I see that I am being criticized and that
they are passing judgement on me without knowing the
circumstances which I cannot reveal, I can only pour out my
grief silently before the tabernacle."[8] This is the lot of all
superiors even in the best abbeys and the most fervent religious
communities. It is their share of the expiation and redemption of mankind. The excessive sensibility of Dom Marmion
made the least opposition particularly painful to him, but his
soul, taking refuge in prayer, soon rose above it all. "I have
suffered a great deal in the last few days, but at the same time,
I have been greatly consoled by the unanimity with which
my monks support me."[9]

The invasion of 1914 came as a cruel disturbance of the
peaceful life of Maredsous. On the 23rd August a wave of
French soldiers flowed around the walls of the abbey, the first
movement of the great battle. It was soon followed by the
whole fourth division of the Belgian army, who were holding
the front at Namur, and were being compelled to retreat by
superior forces. Dom Marmion threw open the gates of his
abbey. The abbatial school and the school of arts were trans-

[7] Letter to a nun of the Dames Anglaises at Bruges, Maredsous, December
12th, 1909.
[8] Letter to D. Thibaut, Maredsous, July 1st, 1910.
[9] Letter, Maredsous, August 25th, 1910.

formed into first-aid stations and received the glorious wounded of the battle of St. Gerard.

After the first confusion was over and the occupation was an accomplished fact, the difficulty of providing for a large number of monks grouped together in a lonely place became insurmountable, and it was necessary to seek some place of refuge for a part of the community. On account of his relations with the English monasteries, Dom Marmion was the obvious person to undertake this difficult task, and it was decided that he should be entrusted with it.

Going to Holland in disguise, he was able to cross to England. There he made every effort to find a place of refuge for his monks where they would be assured of the necessities of life. For a year he wore himself out in this endeavour. He was tempted to lose heart. " I have suffered a great deal in all this business. My rôle as a beggar is very painful to me but I do it for the love of God."[10] Other difficulties arose which were unavoidable in this time of war, when national feelings were aroused and rash judgements were the order of the day. As an Irishman who was a naturalized Belgian and whose major superiors were Germans, he had much to suffer, far from his own Abbey. He was harassed by the atmosphere of suspicion, in addition to much physical suffering and difficulties of every kind: " I am broken in body and scourged in soul by all these annoyances."[11]

Having made provision for his monks, his one desire was to get back to his monastery: " I shall set out in spite of all dangers." [12] At last, at the risk of his life, he managed to reach Maredsous on the 16th May, 1916.

As soon as he heard of his return, Cardinal Mercier, the incarnation of patriotism and of greatness of soul, came to Maredsous to assure him of his undying friendship.

On November 11th, 1918, the bells of the abbey rang out again for victory. Gradually the monastic family gathered again around their Abbot. He greeted his sons as they returned one by one with fatherly affection and great joy, and

[10] Letter, London, January 15th, 1915.
[11] Letter, London, January 28th, 1915.
[12] Letter, Ireland, end of February 1916.

for the rest of his life devoted himself unsparingly to their service, using, like his Master, the irresistible weapon of gentleness in moments of peculiar difficulty.

His influence over his monks was very great: his fatherly kindness won their hearts; his teaching led their souls to God. He was unrivalled as a master of the spiritual life. In this regard he fulfilled admirably one of the most important functions of his office according to the ideal established by St. Benedict, who wishes his Abbot to be "learned in divine law."[13]

The Benedictine Rule attaches great importance to this teaching of the Abbot. It is by means of these intimate, familiar conferences that the father of the monastic family forms his community. "The monastery is almost always a reflection of the Abbot."[14]

Dom Marmion had supreme faith in the sovereign efficacy of the divine word: "You have heard read to-day the prologue of the Rule, which contains the essence of Christian teaching. Every word must be thought out and meditated. There is one point to which I would like to draw your particular attention: *Inclina aurem cordis tui.* Listen carefully to the words of Our Holy Father. He says: "Incline the ear of your heart" so that it may receive eagerly and with the best dispositions: *in corde bono et optimo,* the teaching which is offered to you. This is of capital importance because Christ did not command his apostles to write—most of them wrote nothing—but he said to them: "Go and teach" *Euntes docete.*[15] The words of the preacher are the doctrine of the Word Incarnate; nothing can replace them. St. Paul tells us that for the conversion of souls God chose the "foolishness of our preaching" *stultitia praedicationis.*[16] When God does something we must accept it in the spirit of adoration. Divine Providence has so arranged matters that faith cometh by hearing: *fides ex auditu.*[17] It is the word of the preacher, of him who is sent, *missus*[18] which converts souls. There can be nothing more

---

[13] *Rule,* ch. 64.
[14] Conference, Maredsous, December 26th, 1916.
[15] Matt. xxviii, 19.   [17] Rom. x, 17
[16] I Cor. i, 21.   [18] Luc. iv, 43.

salutary for your souls than the word of God. I could go to the library and copy out from the saints of our Order matter much finer than anything that I can say to you, and come and read it to you. It would be, not the word of the preacher but a mere recitation. But if this word is to do you good, you must, according St. Benedict, "listen with the ears of your heart."[19] You might have the best preachers in the world, a Saint Odo, a Saint Odilon, a St. Paul, or Christ Himself, and it would do you no good if your heart were not rightly disposed. If you listen to the words of your Abbot in a spirit of criticism instead of with faith and humility, they will do you no good, even though he be a saint. My dear brothers, never forget this."[20]

The Rule is the soul of the Benedictine life and from it Dom Marmion drew the most excellent spiritual teaching for his monks. His theological studies and his monastic experience had constituted an excellent preparation for a deep understanding of St. Benedict's work. He realized fully that the Rule is the Gospel of the monk, the very form of his sanctity. It is on it that he will be judged. Dom Marmion professed a passionate devotion to the Rule. The best proof of its excellence, as he used often to say to his monks, is the immense multitude of saints who have been formed by it.

"When I was a novice," he used to say, "the Abbot gave me a copy of the Rule saying: 'you will find everything in this.' At the time I found this hard to believe. Now, after long experience, I am quite convinced of it." It is it which forms in the monk the Christian according to the living image of Christ.[21]

Starting from the maxims of St. Benedict, the Abbot of Maredsous developed his own doctrine on the monastic vows, in which the supernatural and the practical were admirably blended. As the basis of all he took poverty in the full absolute sense of complete renouncement. "*Deus meus et omnia*", St. Francis of Assisi used to say. Poverty is an act

---

[19] Prologue of the Rule.
[20] Conference, Maredsous, May 4th, 1917.
[21] Retreat, Maredsous, September 1916.

of homage paid to God as the infinite good, the supreme beatitude, the sovereign beauty and absolute perfection. The virtue of hope, connoted by the vow of poverty, disposes us to expect from God all the help necessary to arrive at perfect love: *Omnia sperare a Patre.* So also for monastic poverty, our holy Father tells us: *Omnia sperare a Patre monasterii.*[22] This is a vital precept. We must not try to procure for ourselves anything, whatever it may be, by devious means. No, nothing without the permission of the Abbot. The man who manages by little devices to pick up something here and there, is not " expecting everything from the father of the monastery." Why should we fear being stripped of all things? Let us freely renounce all that is superfluous. Let us examine our conscience on this matter with our eyes fixed upon the Poor One of the crib, of Nazareth and of Calvary. We must not be poor merely for show or in appearance; we have vowed to follow Christ in renouncing all things."[23]

Basing his teaching always on the text of the Holy Rule, Dom Marmion explained the full sense and the practical obligations of the vow of chastity. He passed easily from the mystical heights and the sublime significance of monastic virginity to forthright precepts on detachment of the senses and the heart as necessary safeguards of this purity. This versatility is eminently characteristic of his free spontaneous style, moving quickly from one aspect to another and vividly reflecting his own active and rich personality.

Quibus nec corpora licet habere in propria potestate.[24] "The monk cannot dispose of his own body as he wills." As might be expected from a good Irishman and a true father of his family, he approaches the subject with reserve and delicacy but without circumlocution or prudery, in a calm healthy atmosphere, giving his hearers true light from God: "Every man has received from God, with the gift of existence, the right to dispose of his own person and, after the image of the eternal Fatherhood, to establish for himself a home with all the human affection which it implies.

The eternal fruitfulness of the father is expressed in God

---

[22] *Rule*, ch. 23.　　[23] Retreat, Maredsous, September 1916.　　[24] *Rule*, ch. 33.

by that cry of triumph: *Filius meus es tu; Ego hodie genui te*; "'Thou art My Son; this day have I begotten Thee'."[25] Here we have the life of God in this infinite fruitfulness of a God, begetting a Son like to Himself and equal in all respects, united to each other in the same Holy Spirit, Their mutual love. All men have this right. This fruitfulness is something great in men and is a reflection of the fruitfulness of God." Suddenly he introduces into his discourse a picture radiant with the charm of family life. "Let us pay a visit, for example, to our black country. See this collier, a strong man, with muscles of steel and rugged character; he can be quarrelsome, when the occasion arises. Now God has given him the joys of fatherhood. In the evening he comes home. His wife holds up to him the fruit of their love. Immediately this man expands; his face, drawn with weariness, is lit up with a smile; his rough heart becomes tender. These hands, which have been wielding a pickaxe, are stretched out. We have no fear for the tender being which is entrusted to him; it is a reflection of himself; this workman is a father.'[26]

"But why should we have monastic chastity if marriage is something so excellent? There is only one answer: the consecration of one's whole being to Christ. 'We also had the right to establish a home; but freely, deliberately we have willed, have vowed not even to entertain a desire for what we have given up, in order to belong body and soul to Jesus Christ.'[27]

"This is a sublime, superhuman ideal which requires the help of grace: 'Virginity is a gift of God.'[28] And we must adopt the necessary means to safeguard it: humility, mortification, vigilance, the avoidance of dangerous occasions. And then we get many counsels adapted to the detailed circumstances of monastic life: 'The man who indulges in reading of all kinds contrary to morals is almost sure to fall; he will not fall immediately, but he is admitting the spark into his soul and one day the fire will light up. I advise you to mistrust your own strength in this matter as an act of humility. To take risks in reading or in looking at dangerous things

---

[25] Ps. 27.
[26] Retreat, Maredsous, September 1916.
[27] Ibidem.
[28] Ibidem.

without legitimate motive involves an act of pride: it is to
say to God: 'I can be chaste by my own strength.'[29]
"But temptation is not sin. Some of the greatest of the
saints suffered temptation all their lives. 'We are all liable
to temptation. Neither the walls of the monastery nor the
solitude of the hermitage can preserve us from it; our fallen
nature is a part of ourselves. St. Alphonsus de Ligouri, who
left Naples, that city of corruption, with his purity un-
tarnished, was all his life, even in extreme old age, subject to
such temptations that his confessor had to give him absolu-
tion as often as four four times a day, in order to console him.'[30]
A monk who suffers temptations must not be surprised at the
rebellion of his nature. Sin finds its consummation in the
soul. As long as the will does not surrender, there is no
fault."[31]

We see here again the dominant note of Dom Marmion's
teaching which is constantly reappearing: Remember that
we are members of Christ.[32]

The same Christo-centrism is for him the sovereign aid to
the practice of monastic obedience: "If there are times when
obedience presses hard on you, look at the crucifix." Christ
is always the centre of every aspect of his teaching. The Rule
provides Dom Marmion with the simplest everyday maxims
which must guide the life of a community. It is by means of
these inummerable trivial details that a community soul is
formed. "Each individual must be faithful to his duty, which
is the sure expression of the will of God. It is so easy to lapse
into a false mysticism and seek to substitute for one's work a
spiritual life of pure prayer. This is an illusion. The Prior
is responsible before God and before his Abbot for the discipline of the monastery just as the cellarer is responsible for the
material side. We must not say: 'let us carry out this or that
pious exercise and God will see to the rest.' This is an error;
it is to tempt God. If the monastery suffers it will be on the
conscience of him who has neglected his duty, who has not
done what it was his job to do."[33]

[29] Ibidem.
[30] Ibidem.
[31] Ibidem.
[32] I Cor. vi, 15.
[33] Conference, Maredsous, December 22nd, 1916.

The carrying out of these duties must be inspired by love. As might be expected from him with his deep sense of the spiritual, Dom Marmion was constantly insisting on this point. "Our holy father compares the monastery to a workshop, where different trades are being carried on. There is one motive force animating all; if it fails everything is at a standstill. What then, is the motive force of the spiritual life? It is love; and I shall tell you why: Man never acts without a motive, and the more powerful the motive, the more energetically he works. Now love is the most powerful of all motives. Does not God Himself do all things for love? We must try to develop in ourselves the habit of doing everything for love. Then we shall not consider the difficulties. *Ubi amatur non laboratur, aut si laboratur, labor ipse amatur.*[34] Love lightens the burden of work and makes it meritorious. The other good works must take second place. Everyone must practise himself in the virtue which is necessary for him, but he must do it through love and it will come easily to him."[35] As well as these general counsels to the community, there were his personal contacts. Dom Marmion knew how to approach a monk whom he saw to be in difficulty or disturbed. There was nothing formal or strained in the relations between the Abbot and his monks. When one of them suffered a bereavement or went to Rome to pursue his studies, or if anyone, for any reason, was absent for a time from the monastery Dom Marmion would write to them with cordial affection. Whether it was joy or sorrow, he wished to associate himself with all that happened to his monks. His fatherly heart was sensitive to everything that affected any one of them. The dominant note in his personal relations with them was his inexhaustible kindness. His fatherly spirit seemed to increase with the years. "A line to tell you that your wishes are granted. I can understand something of the pleasure our heavenly Father experiences in granting us what we ask Him, by the joy it gives me to give you pleasure. 'If you then being evil know how to give good gifts to your children, how much more will your Father, who is in heaven, give you what you ask Him.'"[36]

[34] St. Augustine.   [35] Conference, Maredsous, May 1917.   [36] Matt. vii, 11.

It would be impossible to give an adequate picture of the pre-eminent goodness of Dom Marmion, his great and noble sensibility, his exceptionally quick sympathy or his kindness which never counted the cost and which, though it was perhaps abused at times, won him the eternal affection of the best of his monks.

As well as his commentaries on the Rule on Mondays and Fridays, Dom Marmion spoke to his community every Sunday and feast day. He drew from the liturgical cycle and the gospel of the day the subject matter of those magnificent conferences in which he gave all that was best in him as a doctor and contemplative. The great figure of Christ dominated his thought and stood out in striking relief. His accent of conviction, his radiant faith and his ardent passion for the Son of God burst out in these talks and raised them at times to the level of true eloquence, that eloquence which can come only from the heart of an apostle or a saint. We find the echo of it in some of the best pages of *Christ in His Mysteries*. What a wealth of light and grace it must have contained for those who had the privilege of hearing his living voice! "The doctrine is not mine," Dom Marmion used to protest, "*non est mea doctrina*. I have drawn it from the Gospels, the Epistles, from tradition and the Holy Rule."[37] In fact, through the rich subject matter of his conferences and conversations, we can perceive his whole soul, the soul of a monk, an apostle and a contemplative, which expressed itself, communicating to his eager and enthusiastic words the whole force of his personality. He had the gift of inspiring the same enthusiasm in the souls of others through the medium of those fundamental themes which were constantly reappearing in his discourses: the grandeur of our divine sonship, and the infinite riches of the grace of adoption in Jesus Christ; the supernatural character of our sanctity; faith, the foundation of our life of union with Christ. Then we come to the great monastic virtues: humility and the spirit of mortification; compunction of heart; obedience, the supreme good of monks; absolute fidelity to the observance, a fidelity free from the pharisaical spirit but inspired by love. And finally and above all, con-

[37] Retreat, Maredsous, September 1916.

fidence in the infinite mercies of the Saviour to assist our weakness and an absolute reliance on the divine mercy.

Above all, the Abbot's object was to raise souls up to Christ so that "with Him, through Him and in Him" he might bring them to the bosom of the Father.[38] The sacrifice of the Mass was the culminating point of his abbatial life in which he accomplished his mission as pontiff and mediator between the community and God. Except for the last years of his life when he was disabled by illness, he was always present for the Office in choir, profoundly recollected and united with Christ in the spirit of adoration. "Do you know what I feel most, when I have to be away from the monastery? The loss of the Conventual Mass. It seems so splendid a thing to offer *together* to the heavenly Father the immolation of His Divine Son."[39] His greatest joy was to celebrate pontifical Mass himself, surrounded by his monks. This was for him a sacred time when, in communion with the eternal Priest, the whole monastic community, assembled round their head, were one in Christ.

World-wide Influence

The personality of Dom Columba Marmion, which had already made itself felt as Prior of Mont-César, came into much greater prominence on his election as head of the great abbey of Maredsous. His influence extended far and wide, in Belgium, Ireland, England and throughout the whole Benedictine Order.

His gifts as a preacher of retreats and his exceptional capacity as a master of the spiritual life opened up for him an extensive apostolate in Benedictine monasteries, and among secular priests and communities of nuns. He was to be found in Louvain, Liège, Bruges and in England, at the invitation of the Bishops and of his Eminence Cardinal Bourne, who invited him on several occasions of national importance to his cathedral at Westminister.

He played an important part in the celebrated conversion

[38] John i, 18.   [39] *Un maître de la vie Spirituelle*, p. 227.

of the monks of Caldey, which constituted a unique event in
the history of the Church. It was Dom Marmion who preached
the retreat before their abjuration and reception into the
Catholic Church. "I have just arrived here and I am really
delighted. All the monks are charming. The bishop of the
diocese, Mgr. Mostyn, is arriving to-morrow. They will all be
baptized, reconciled with the Church and confirmed. They
are unanimous in their faith and in their desire to be reconciled with Rome. . . . .

"To-morrow the bishop, Abbot Butler of Downside, and I
will consider the situation and see what can be done. The
Holy Father has sent them a cordial telegram of paternal
greeting. The whole of England is moved by the affair. . . .
I have just celebrated Mass in their magnificent choir and I
have given them a conference, text: *Cantate Domino Canti-*
cum novum, laus eius in Ecclesia Sanctorum.[40] "Sing ye to
the Lord a new canticle; let his praise be in the church of the
saints."[41]

On 5th March Mgr. Mostyn received their abjuration and
two days afterwards that of the thirty-seven Anglican nuns of
St. Bride. On the 6th March Dom Marmion sent his Prior at
Maredsous an account of this sensational conversion. "So
much has happened since my last letter. I would like to be
able to tell you all about it. It is the most important step
towards the conversion of England since the Oxford movement."[42]

On the 29th June Dom Marmion was again on the island
for the taking of the habit and for the erection of the house
into a Benedictine monastery.

The Abbot of Maredsous was frequently on the road in
obedience to calls from bishops or orders from his major
superiors and in the execution of important missions. His
correspondence reveals to us a life of constant overwork:
"Chapter General at Beuron in July, a retreat in Hayward's
Heath in August, a liturgical congress here in the same month
and then a Marian Congress with Cardinal Mercier. I have

[40] Ps. cxlix, 1.
[41] Letter to Dom Robert, March 3rd, 1913.
[42] Ibidem, March 6th, 1913.

F

all sorts of other invitations which I shall have to refuse."[43]
It was in vain that he tried to extricate himself from these
engagements. Writing from England, whither he had been
summoned by Cardinal Bourne, he says: "I am really upset
and saddened by being away, and now you know that I have
to go to Rome."[44] His personal influence was extending every
day and now his fame was spread throughout the world by the
publication of his famous trilogy: *Christ, the Life of the Soul;
Christ in His Mysteries*, and *Christ, the Ideal of the Monk*.

Consummation in Christ

The publication of these three works revealed the secret of
the profound influence which the Abbot of Maredsous exercised over souls—it was his intimacy with Christ.

In the first years of his monastic life, Dom Columba had
applied himself fervently to the practice of humility, of
compunction of heart, and of religious obedience. He
laboured faithfully, sometimes to the point of heroism, by
means of mortification of the senses and of the heart to arrive
at complete detachment. During this time at Louvain the
work of purification had been accelerated by marvellous graces
of union. Now, in the evening of his life, his abbatiate was
marked by great trials both exterior and interior which he
endured with complete confidence in the merits of the Saviour,
abandoning himself unreservedly to the goodness and mercy
of the heavenly Father; it was the period of his consummation
in Christ.

It remains for us to consider this final and most sublime
stage of his spiritual journey.

As the difficulties of life increased, his soul tended to lose
itself more and more in Christ. "Our Lord inspires me with
a great attraction to lay myself completely and continuously at
the feet of the Word Incarnate. I wish to imitate His sacred
Humanity in its union, its submission and its absolute dependence on the Word. Help me to realize this ideal, for it includes
everything. Once the Father sees a soul united in this manner

[43] Letter to a nun of Tyburn, Mardesous, February 6th, 1912.
[44] Letter to Dom Robert, Prior, September 6th, 1912.

with His Word there are no graces or favours which He will not bestow upon it. . . . . The Sacred Humanity is the way . . . . It is of infinite efficacy to unite us to the Word. Let us then be saints for His glory. 'In this is My Father glorified, that you bring forth very much fruit.' *In hoc clarificatus est Pater meus, si fructum plurimum afferatis.*"[45,46]

The exercise of his office brought him nearer to God. " I am much more closely united to Our Lord than I was at the beginning and He is clearly blessing my efforts to govern His house in accordance with His divine will. I feel especially drawn by Jesus to dwell with Him in the bosom of the Father, *in sinu Patris,* but this requires great fidelity and great self-denial."

God, however, left him to bear his bodily infirmities and the ups and downs of his spirit. " I am like a poor trapped beast not finding a moment of peace in the midst of a thousand cares and I am subject to such exhaustion that often during the Conventual Mass, I have to make a great effort not to fall asleep on the floor. . . . Sometimes I am troubled by the thought that I ought to resign on account of these fits of exhaustion and sleepiness which make me incapable of prayer or work. If they get any worse I do not know how I can face my constant duties and responsibilities."[47]

He was becoming extremely stout, but, though he became heavier in body, his soul continued to soar towards God. "Perfect happiness, the supreme joy is to be found *in sinu Patris* and Jesus is the way which leads us there. Without Him we can do nothing.[48] 'No man goes to the Father but by Him.'[49] Let us live in Jesus."[50] In the midst of innumerable troubles incident to the government and administration of a great abbey there appears suddenly in his correspondence luminous gems of dogma, which reveal the soul of a saint eager to consummate his union with God. " For my part· I am very close to Our Lord. He is always present in my heart and I

[45] John xv, 8.
[46] Letter to a Carmelite, Maredsous, November 8th, 1910.
[47] Letter to a nun of Tyburn Convent, February 11th, 1911.
[48] John xv, 5.
[49] John xiv, 6.
[50] Letter to the Carmelite nuns of Louvain, Beuron, June 5th, 1913.

confide to Him all my cares and all my preoccupations. I derive great consolation and strength from the reflection that he is constantly present before His Father in a dual capacity. As the only begotten Son, He is of His own right *in sinu Patris*, as the adorer, the lover etc. As Head of His own mystical body, *semper apparet vultui Deo pro nobis*: 'He is always present before God *for us*.'[51] He is there as *Jesus* for us, for our salvation, *Propter nos homines et propter nostram salutem*, always living to make intercession for us, *semper vivens ad interpellandum pro nobis*.[52] He presents for us to His Father this sacrifice accomplished once but always existing. United to Him, we enter as of right into the *sanctuarium exauditionis* where all our petitions receive favourable hearing."[53]

His spiritual life was becoming ever more closely identified with the relation of the soul of Jesus to His Father. On the occasion of a retreat at Maredret, he chose as his subject the life and all the activity of Jesus considered as emanating from the contemplation of His soul which beheld constantly the Face of His Father as the model of a life of Faith, finding all things in the habitual contemplation of God, in union with the soul of Christ.[54] Thus, with the passage of years and the trials of life, Dom Marmion advanced farther every day in union with Christ. "It is by successive detachments that we arrive in the end at loving Him as our ALL."[55]

The development of his life of union with Christ was not a sudden tranformation; it was rather a constant and ever-increasing fidelity. Dom Marmion was the embodiment of the essentially normal type of sanctity: 'I have never received any extraordinary grace that I know of: no interior voices, visions, ecstasies; not even that domination of the spirit which prevents all activity; nothing of the kind. I feel no attraction towards them. It seems to me that the grace of adoption, this germ received in baptism, strengthened in confirmation and nourished by the Holy Eucharist, is constantly developing

[51] Heb. ix, 24.
[52] Heb. vii, 25.
[53] Letter to a Carmelite nun, Maredsous, July 20th, 1914.
[54] Ibidem, December 18th, 1916.
[55] Ibidem, May 1st, 1918.

through Christ." This is a splendid confidence which illumin-ates retrospectively the spiritual journey of Dom Marmion. He followed the normal way of all baptized souls. Through all the stages of his existence he had submitted himself to the guidance of Providence and had suffered himself to be transformed ever more completely into Christ. Far from discouraging him, his own wretchedness served always to cast him into the arms of Christ the Saviour: " I am sixty years old to-day. The mass of my sins and my ingratitude has been swallowed up in the infinite abyss of the mercy of the Father."[56]

During the last years his spiritual life became still more simple. " My interior life is very simple. During my stay here Our Lord has united me very closely to Himself in simple faith. I am convinced that this is the road by which He wishes to lead me. I never experience any sensible consola-tions. I do not desire them. I have moments of illumination, sudden perceptions, as it were, of the depths of revealed truth. I feel a special attraction for compunction. The thought of the father of the prodigal son, of the good Samaritan, of Jesus with Magdalen at His feet, fills me with compunction and with confidence. My tendency is to find everything in Jesus and through Him. It is the way marked out for us by the Father. It is by Him that we must go to the Father."[57]

As the evening of life approaches, it is Christ alone Who has an attraction for him: " I find Him everywhere and in every-thing. He is the Alpha and the Omega of everything. I am so poor, so wretched in myself and so rich in Him. To Him be all glory of all times."[58]

It is the hour of the final consummation. On the thirtieth of January 1923, after much suffering and with complete abandonment to the divine mercy: *Deus meus, misericordia mea,*[59] the soul of Dom Marmion departed to join Christ for all eternity in the bosom of the Father.

[56] Ibidem, May 1st, 1918.
[57] Letter to a Carmelite nun, Beauplateau, September 25th, 1918.
[58] Letter to D. Winefreda Kraemer, Maredsous, June 26th, 1921.
[59] Ps. lvii, 20.

II

OUR LIFE IN CHRIST

Our predestination in Christ – Christ the
"adequate" cause of our sanctity – The
fundamental axiom – The Christian antithesis: death and life – Death to sin – Life
in God – Transformation into Christ – Life
of union with Christ – In sinu Patris

*To die to sin in order to live for
God. The whole of Christianity
lies in that death and that life.*

II

OUR LIFE IN CHRIST

THIS absolute domination of the soul of Dom Marmion by Christ explains the whole tendency of his spirituality. In him the saint and the doctor were united. He had entered into the depths of the mystery of Christ, in the light of a grace personal to himself, often inspired by St. Paul, and under the guidance of the teaching of St. Thomas Aquinas. Under the combined influence of these two great masters his spiritual doctrine has achieved the universality of the divine plan, embracing in its organic unity the whole economy of salvation and of the sanctification of souls in Christ.

Our Predestination in Christ

The fundamental intuition which was to become the key-note of his spiritual doctrine was inspired by the celebrated passage of St. Paul in which the apostle gives us his concept of what the Christian life meant. It is Dom Marmion himself who gives us the reference. "All this sublime plan is splendidly exposed to us in this first chapter of the Ephesians: 'Blessed be the God and Father of Our Lord Jesus Christ who hath blessed us with spiritual blessings in heavenly places in Christ. As He chose us in Him before the foundation of the world that we should be holy and unspotted in His sight in charity who hath predestined us unto the adoption of children through Jesus Christ unto Himself'."[1,2]

While Elizabeth of the Holy Trinity may find in this text her supreme vocation to the "praise of glory", Dom Columba is struck by the mystery of our predestination of adoption in

[1] Eph. i, 3-5.   [2] Retreat, undated.

89

Jesus Christ. His theological mind concentrated on this central point. He appreciated the full significance of the word "predestination". It signifies an irrevocable decree of God which controls the whole organization of the world and the whole plan of our salvation. It is God's will "to re-establish all things in Christ that are in heaven and on earth ",[3] or according to the Greek text, which Dom Marmion preferred: "It is God's will to make Christ the chief, the head of all creation." His contemplative soul is overwhelmed by this truth. Henceforth he always thought of Christ as occupying the first place in the universe. So, with his living faith illuminated by the gifts of the Holy Ghost, he realized the unique and universal rôle of the Word Incarnate in the redemption of the world. He saw in Him the exemplary, the meritorious and the instrumental cause of all sanctity. Now fully enlightened, he has a clear concept of the universe; a concept which is identified with the divine plan, in which Christ is everything.

His whole spiritual doctrine is derived from this concept. The following are its essential principles: It was the original plan of the Holy Trinity in the creation of man to form him according to their image and likeness: *Faciamus hominem ad imaginem nostram.*[4] After the fall of Adam, God willed to restore all things in His Son. It was in this way that Christ became the centre of the divine plan.

God the Father communicates to Him His divine life by way of eternal generation. The Word Incarnate, having received in His humanity an infinite plenitude of grace, pours it forth on men in proportion to their willingness to "receive "[5] the only begotten Son of the Father by a lively faith and through the sacraments. All Christian holiness consists therefore in letting oneself be transformed into Christ who has become our wisdom, our sanctification and our redemption.[6]

An invaluable note, in his own handwriting, gives us the summary in which this Benedictine theologian has set out the essentials of his spiritual doctrine: "Let us study the divine plan in all its purity and all its beauty, for our whole spiritual

[3] Eph. i, 10.   [4] Gen. i, 26.   [5] John i, 12.   [6] I Cor. 1, 30.

life depends on the adequacy of our grasp of these first principles and our establishing them as the foundation of our sanctity. In order to understand the divine plan we must consider that the sanctity to which we are called is not a merely natural sanctity, not a simple observance of the moral law. The sanctity to which we are called is supernatural life. Now this divine life, which finds its full development in the beatific vision, comes down to us from the Father, through Jesus Christ: *Sicut Pater habet vitam in semetipso, sic dedit et Filio habere vitam in semetipso.*[7]

"*Et de plenitudine eius omnes accepimus.*"[8] The Father communicates it to His Son in all its fulness by the eternal generation and then to the Word Incarnate by the hypostatic union. Let us consider for a moment Jesus Christ, *auctor et consummator salutis;*[9] *in quo sunt omnes thesauri sapientiae et SCIENTIAE Dei;*[10] *In quo inhabitat omnis plenitudo divinitatis corporaliter.*[11] He is '*perfectus Deus* and *perfectus homo*'. But this divine life which He possesses in all its fulness, elevates all His human activity, makes it theandric, and finds expression in the radiance of all the virtues, like a ray of light which, passing through the prism, emerges in a multitude of colours. That is why He is the Holy of Holies: *Tu solus sanctus Jesu Christe* (Gloria in excelsis), and filled with all the gifts of the Holy Ghost.

"But it is not for Himself alone that Jesus has received this divine life. He is also *our* sanctity: *Christus factus est nobis sapientia a Deo.*[12] He is the head and we are the members. He has come to communicate His divine life to us. *Ego veni ut vitam habeant et abundantius habeant.*[13] *Ego sum vita.*[14] This, then, is the divine plan: the divine life is communicated in all its fulness to Jesus Christ and by Him to His members: *de plenitudine eius omnes accepimus.*[15]

"How does Jesus Christ communicate His divine life to us? He does so by making us, like Himself, children of God. If Jesus is the temple of the divinity, if He is the Holy of Holies, the source of all this is His divine sonship. In like

---

[7] John v, 26.
[8] John i, 16.
[9] Heb. xii, 2.
[10] Col. ii, 3.
[11] Col. ii, 9.
[12] I Cor. i, 30.
[13] John x, 10.
[14] John xiv, 6.
[15] John i, 16.

manner the source of all our graces and all the gifts of God is our status as the adopted children of God. *Praedestinavit nos in adoptionem filiorum per Jesus Christum.*[16] By reason of this adoption we are no more strangers and foreigners;[17] we have become heirs of God and joint heirs with Christ.[18]

" This adoption derives from faith in Jesus Christ and the sacrament of this faith is Baptism. This faith in Jesus Christ is not a mere theoretic admission of His divinity; it is a practical faith which casts us in adoration at His feet like the man born blind: ' I believe, Lord. And falling down, he adored Him.'[19] It is a faith which flowers into hope and charity, and which increases steadily until it becomes the life and sole inspiration of our activity: ' I live now, not I, but Christ liveth in me '." [20, 21]

These vast perspectives in which the spiritual thought of Dom Marmion found its development are in the fullest harmony with the Pauline concept of the world.

With decisive vigour and a touch of humour he deplores the tendency of men to seek to become " the architects of their own perfection."[22]

" Many people, even religious and priests, have a false idea of sanctity. They confuse real sanctity with the method, systems, and practices with which men have surrounded it, *traditiones hominum;*[23] and, as a result, the yoke which Our Lord declared to be sweet and light becomes unbearable. This is a very grave evil. But still more grave is the tendency of these people to substitute all this system of practices and methods for the doctrine which Jesus Christ preached, for the Law which He gave us."[24]

" It is not for us to work out our own sanctity; we must adapt ourselves to the divine plan. We must go to God in His way, rather than in our own."[25]

Whether Dom Marmion was speaking to the ordinary faithful, to contemplative nuns, to religious or to priests, the policy he proposed to them was the same: Christ. " The plan of the

[16] Eph. i, 5.
[17] Eph. ii, 19.
[18] Rom. viii, 17.
[19] John ix, 38.
[20] Gal. ii, 20.
[21] Retreat, Maredsous, 1909.
[22] Retreat, Erdington, 1902.
[23] Col. ii, 8.
[24] Conference, 1901.
[25] Retreat, Maredsous, 1909.

Eternal Father, the mystery hidden in God from ages and generations[26] is to 're-establish all things',[27] to sanctify the world by His Son. Jesus Christ is the only 'way'[28] by which one may go to the Father."[29]

This is, in broad outline, the magnificent synthesis of this apostle of Christ. It is in the bosom of the Trinity, in its eternal source, that he has discovered the supreme model of our sanctity. He likes to dwell on the immense current of divine life proceeding from the Father through the Son under the impulse of the Holy Spirit, flowing first in all its fulness to the Word Incarnate through the humanity of Jesus, into the whole Church, and reaching, through the centuries, each individual member of the mystical body. It is the glorious vision which has in it something of the infinitude of the divine plan.

It never entered the mind of Dom Marmion to map out a new way of perfection or another approach for the soul to God. For him there was only one "way" of sanctity: Christ. It was enough to lose oneself in Him in accordance with the designs of God. Every man has his destiny fixed in Christ by virtue of his membership of the mystical body. The whole Christ embraces in Himself all the individual vocations. God the Father contemplates us in His only-begotten Son, united in one economy of salvation. The same decree of predestination determined the Incarnation of the Word and our adoption in Jesus Christ.

In this mystery of our predestination to divine adoption we touch on the inmost secret of our destiny. It was the special grace of Dom Marmion to have sounded, with penetrating intuition, all the depths of this mystery and to have exposed its immense importance for the sanctification of souls. This fundamental truth is the key to his spiritual doctrine.

Christ the "adequate" cause of our sanctity

In the light of this truth we can clearly understand his spiritual doctrine. Christ is for him the one source of all

[26] Col. i, 26.
[27] Eph. i, 10.
[28] John xiv, 6.
[29] Retreat to Priests, Louvain, 1898.

sanctity.   All his teaching is built up around this one idea with a remarkable power of synthesis.   Up to the very end of his life he never tired of expounding to the most varied audiences what he called "that radiant principle" of St. Thomas Aquinas which shows us Christ as the "adequate cause of our sanctity."[30]   "The holy doctor reminds us, following the doctrine of St. Paul, that Our Lord is for us the Alpha and the Omega; in other words that He is for us the absolute all, and that, apart from Him, there is no spiritual life.   Has not Jesus Himself said to us in the Gospel: 'Without me you can do nothing.'[31]   'Nihil': absolutely nothing.   All that we can do on our own, our plans, our methods of mental prayer, our expedients, all these are entirely useless if they are not based on Christ, for Christ is everything in our sanctification.   As St. Thomas says, Christ is the exemplary cause and model of our sanctity.   He is the meritorious cause which gives all the actions of our life their value, and the efficient cause which operates our sanctity.   We have therefore in Christ the perfect model of our perfection.   He has paid all our debts.   He merited infinitely more than was necessary for our redemption: *copiosa apud eum redemptio*.[32]   He died for us, and He received from the Father the power to apply to us the fruit of His Passion: 'All power is given to me in heaven and in earth.'[33,34]

We know the major importance of the mystery of predestination in the Thomist synthesis.   Christ holds the first place in the divine decrees.   Through the hypostatic union, by reason of His divine Sonship, He is at the head of the universe for which He has revealed the final purpose.   As head of a mystical body, of which the angels themselves are members, He is the Redeemer of mankind and the cause of our sanctity by way of model and of satisfaction, of merit and impetration and likewise as the final and efficient cause.   "And you are Christ's and Christ is God's."[35]

There are three aspects of this vast concept of Aquinas

[30] Retreat to priests, Westminster, 1919; retreat, Maredsous, September 1919.
[31] John xv, 5.   [34] Conference, Mardret, October 20th, 1909.
[32] Ps. cxxix, 7.   [35] I Cor. iii, 23.
[33] Matt. xxviii, 18.

which the contemplative mind of Dom Marmion has made especially his own and which he has developed marvellously in *Christ the Life of the Soul*, like a true doctor of spirituality: the Word Incarnate is the exemplary, the meritorious and the instrumental cause of our salvation. But while it is the intellectual genius of St. Thomas which provided for Dom Marmion the directive principles of his thought, it was always in the Scriptures and especially in the writings of his beloved St. Paul that he found the final inspiration of his doctrine.

We see this clearly in his concept of Christ as the exemplary cause of our sanctity. Through the medium of the Pauline formulas he sees with the mind of a theologian the prototype of our perfection in Jesus Christ. He rises effortlessly as usual to the greatest heights of spiritual wisdom on the sense of our configuration with the Word Incarnate, reverting constantly to his favourite text; "For whom He foreknew He also predestined to be made conformable to the image of His Son."[36] All our perfection lies in that. The eternal Father bestows His graces on us in proportion as He finds His Son in us. When God sees a soul completely transformed into His Son He is drawn to it; He communicates His own being to that soul unreservedly: this is the secret of the gifts of God to us."[37]

The more closely we resemble Christ, the holier we are. The imitation of Christ is the fundamental law and the standard of all sanctity. This does not mean that we should aim at a servile reproduction of the acts and gestures of Jesus, but rather that we try to make our own His inner sentiments. Dom Marmion makes gentle fun of M. Camus for trying to imitate St. Francis de Sales even in his outward bearing and his deliberate manner of speaking.[38] For him the whole effort of the interior life was directed towards modelling himself interiorly on Jesus and identifying himself more and more closely with the sentiments of Jesus towards His Father.

Christ is the ideal Christian. "He is a revelation of divine sanctity in human form: God adapted to our comprehension. The object of Christianity must be the reproduction of this

[36] Rom, viii, 29.
[37] Conference, Maredret, November 17th, 1909.
[38] Conference, Maredret, November 26th, 1909.

model of all perfection: *Christianus alter Christus.* The true
Christian is another Christ."[39]

We must not think of Jesus merely as a model. By reason
of His infinite merits He is a permanent source of sanctity.
"The older I grow, the more I have to deal with souls, the
more clearly I can see the necessity of making them understand how rich they are in Jesus Christ. Above all else it is
essential to make them realize that in Christ they have all
riches and all the means necessary to arrive at a very high
perfection."[40]

This vital truth was one of those which had the greatest
influence in the personal life of Dom Marmion. The unity
of the mystical body is the key to the doctrine of our redemption. According to the Pauline doctrine, with which the
Abbot of Maredsous was so familiar, the Head and the members form one body. We are Christ. Each one of the actions
of Jesus, our Head, has a direct bearing on the plan of our
salvation. It is as though each one of us, in his own right,
had merited and been redeemed in Christ. "All the infinite
riches of His Sacred Heart are ours, more truly ours than
anything that we possess in this world, provided that we are
united to Him by divine grace. I would like to imprint this
truth in your heart in letters of gold."[41]

"There is nothing which we cannot obtain provided that
our faith is at the level of these riches which we possess in
Christ."[42] Why then should we let ourselves be discouraged
by our personal deficiencies. Is not Christ there to provide
the remedy for all these? "However great our wretchedness,
our infidelity, our weakness, provided we remain closely
united to Jesus by faith and love, we shall triumph over all."[43]

We can imagine the immense consolation that this teaching
gave to souls. The conviction with which it was expressed
gave extraordinary force to his teaching. One felt that the
intimate drama of his own life was being revealed in his con-

[39] Conference to priests, Louvain, December 1905.
[40] Conference, Maredret, April 18th, 1911.
[41] Letter to nun. Louvain, July 2nd, 1896.
[42] Conference, Maredret, December 23rd, 1913.
[43] Retreat to priests, Louvain, October 1898.

fessions of powerlessness and wretchedness with the sudden contrasts of transports of love and unbounded confidence in Jesus Christ. How many of his listeners—I can vouch for it—were profoundly moved by his teaching! "What then can prevent us from achieving sanctity? I have had thirty years experience as a priest and I want to tell you what my experience with souls has taught me."

"Our spiritual life must gravitate around two poles: on the one hand the intimate conviction that without the help of God we are incapable of sanctity; on the other hand the conviction that, with the help of God, we can attain the most sublime sanctity.

"St. Paul understood this clearly. He declares that we are not sufficient to think anything of ourselves,[44] but he acknowledges that with the grace of God we can do all things: 'I can do all things in Him who strengtheneth me'."[45, 46]

But the truth which impressed Dom Marmion most forcibly was the instrumental rôle of the humanity of Christ. It is this which gives its intense realism to his spiritual doctrine and which constituted a characteristic feature of his teaching. More perhaps than any other theologian he brought this truth into the realm of practical reality.

"All those infinite riches which the Father confided to His Son and which Jesus merited for us He applies to our souls by way of instrumental cause."[47] "Our Lord is always the principal factor in our sanctification: 'Without me you can do nothing.'[48] Christ dwelling in the centre of our soul devotes Himself to effecting our transformation into Him. The Son of God, the Word, is the supreme ideal; Christ labours continuously to impress on us that image of God of which He is the perfect example."[49]

With a clearness of thought which is rare, Dom Marmion had grasped the unique part played by Christ in our spiritual life. Many souls regard Christ merely as a model to be

[44] II Cor. iii, 5.
[45] Phil. iv, 13.
[46] Conference, Maredret, November 16th, 1917.
[47] Retreat, Maredret, November 1901.
[48] John xv, 5.
[49] Retreat, Maredret, December 1905.

G

imitated; for him Christ was everything. "You often find spiritual authors neglecting this fundamental truth," said Dom Marmion, "it seems, so to speak, to have escaped them. On the other hand, when you study St. Thomas, you see that this great doctor, so skilled in penetrating the eternal truths, laid particular stress on this point. He tells us that in Jesus we have the model of all the virtues, the meritorious cause of all graces, the instrumental cause of our sanctification and the adequate cause of all sanctity. The older I get the more clearly I see the importance of teaching souls that they possess in Jesus Christ all riches necessary to arrive at the highest perfection."[50]

The Fundamental Axiom

These dogmatic truths, which are propounded by the conventional theologian as purely abstract theses of the schools, took on an intense vitality in the soul of Dom Marmion which makes the figure of Christ stand out in striking relief. For him Christ was a veritable presence, the source of light and of life.

Hence the fundamental axiom of his teaching:

"ALL OUR SANCTITY CONSISTS IN BECOMING BY GRACE WHAT JESUS CHRIST IS BY NATURE, THE CHILD OF GOD."[51]

Another truth no less important follows from this: the standard of our spiritual life corresponds to the degree of our conformity with Christ. "The more God sees His Son in each one of us, the more abundantly He showers His gifts on us."[52] For God includes in the same act of love His Son and the multitude of His brethren who form one body with Him.

The exceptional grace of Dom Marmion lay in his return to this appreciation of the simplicity of the divine plan and it was this that gave to his spiritual doctrine its exceptional vigour. *Omnia restaurare in Christo.*[53] Other spiritual authors may surpass him in the depth of their analysis and descriptions of phases of the mystical life; none has equalled him in the

---

[50] Conference, Maredret, April 18th, 1911.   [52] Ibidem.
[51] Retreat, Hayward's Heath, August 1905.   [53] Eph. i, 10.

force of his Christo-centrism. "If I were asked in what the spiritual life consisted, I would answer: Christ."[54]

The Christian Antithesis

Like St. Paul, Dom Marmion based the whole edifice of his spiritual doctrine on the most important event of Christianity: the death and resurrection of Jesus. In his moral and mystical theology as in his concept of Christian dogma, Christ was everything. It did not occur to him to construct his system around an abstract idea. He starts from an historical fact: Christ died and rose again. The Christian life appears to him as a participation in the death and resurrection of the Saviour, as a prolongation of Christ. "Just as the whole existence of Christ can be summed up in the words: 'He died to sin. . . . he liveth unto God', *mortuus est semel* and *vivit Deo*[55] so also are they a summary of the Christian life."[56] The whole of Christianity can be reduced to this mystery of death and life. It is just this return to the essentials of Christianity which assured for the doctrine of Dom Marmion its widespread influence and its prominence.

This basic antithesis is itself derived from a still more fundamental law of religion. All sanctity implies of necessity a double element: the one of separation, the other of union. It is of the very nature of things that one can only approach God by separating oneself from all created things. Our condition as sinners has accentuated this twofold aspect, negative and positive, of this inevitable conflict which lies at the heart of all sanctity. Death and life constitute the two correlative and complementary plans of the Christian life.

A note which is undated, but which goes back certainly to the first years of his apostolic work as a monk, gives us, in the form of a plan for a retreat, the secret of this intuition which formed the structure and basis of Dom Marmion's spirituality. It is the scheme of *Christ the Life of the Soul, Christ the Ideal of the Monk* and *Christ the Ideal of the Priest*. There are two main divisions of the retreat:

[54] Letter undated.   [55] Rom. vi, 10.
[56] Retreat, Maredret, November 1901.

Firstly, "death with Jesus to sin, to all imperfections and to ourselves."

Secondly, "Resurrection with Him to a new life."

"We see here," remarks his biographer, Dom Thibaut, "the whole framework of his fundamental work in all its clearness and simplicity, in all its strength and power."[57]

The Abbot of Maredsous remained absolutely faithful to this initial programme, from which he drew a maxim of immense importance in the direction of souls: "The degree of this death to sin is the measure of our progress in the way of perfection."[58]

Death to Sin

No form of moral teaching can ignore the struggle against evil. Spiritual combat is the law of our fallen nature and is rooted in the very heart of the mystery of our Redemption. To be holy means to achieve victory in one's own soul over the forces of evil.

Considering sin as a spiritual father rather than as a psychologist, Dom Marmion regarded it above all as the great obstacle to union with God and as an offence against love. "Sin is the refusal of the creature to his God who invites him to union with Him."[59] Nothing in the world should persuade us to consent to commit the least venial sin "even to avert the greatest misfortunes: wars, sickness, etc. . . . All the sufferings of men considered in themselves would not suffice to blot out a single venial sin."[60] As for mortal sin, it "renders the soul incapable of all union with God. Man turns away from God. Were he to die in that state, his will would be fixed irrevocably, for all eternity alienated from God."[61] It has cost the blood of a God to secure its expiation and pardon.

Under the influence of books, the cinema, the radio and the whole atmostphere of a pagan civilization, our modern mentality has lost the sense of sin. The principal reason is that we have no longer any appreciation of God. Dom

[57] A Master of the Spiritual Life.
[58] Retreat, Maredret, 1898.
[59] Retreat, Maredret, November 1901.
[60] Retreat, Maredret, 1898.
[61] Plan for retreat, undated.

Marmion's faith had impressed on his soul a vivid horror of sin and his experience as a priest had given him a full understanding of its effects. This explains the fundamental importance in his spiritual doctrine of the sacrament and virtue of penance, the remedies for sin. He prepared himself for confession with the same intensity as for the holy sacrifice of the Mass and always professed a special devotion for this sacrament.

It was doubtless due to this earnest devotion that he derived such exceptional fruits from this sacrament. "Besides conferring sanctifying grace, the sacrament of penance weakens the roots of sin in the soul and gives a greater strength and stability for good. It gives the intelligence a supernatural light to see the beauty of virtue and the ugliness of sin, and communicates to the will an increase of strength to fight against the attractions of evil and to remain faithful to God. If there were no obstacle on our part each confession would so weaken the reign of sin in our souls and would establish us so firmly in virtue that we would be, in accordance with the doctrine of St. Paul, truly 'dead to sin but alive unto God.'[62] "Every time that we make a good confession the infinite merits of Jesus Christ are offered to the eternal Father; and St. Gregory declares that by a good confession we give more glory to God than our sins have given Him offence."[63]

When Dom Marmion, in the spirit of a skilled theologian, takes up one by one the traditional divisions of the sacrament of penance, his analysis is permeated with the thought of Christ. "By these acts of the penitent we are associated with the inmost sentiments of Christ expiating the sins of the world. We participate in the expiatory sufferings of the Agony of Gethsemane."[64]

Even when the sin has been forgiven some of the effects remain; there are evil, vicious inclinations deeply rooted in the sinful soul which constitute a serious obstacle to perfect union. 'We must carry on a vigorous struggle against all these unhealthy tendencies; otherwise we are building on

---

[62] Rom. vi, 11.
[63] Retreat to priests, Louvain, October 1898.
[64] Retreat, Maredret, 1901.

sand. How many apostasies, even among religious and priests,
may be explained by the failure to fight generously against
oneself. The crash comes suddenly, but pride, self-love and
sensuality have long undermined the souls."[65]

It is therefore of primary importance to mortify ourselves.
"The true disciples of Christ, following the example of their
master, 'have crucified their flesh with its vices and con-
cupiscences.'[66] The primary object of mortification, its direct,
immediate object, is to guarantee us control over our evil
instincts and to re-establish the equilibrium destroyed by
sin."[67]

The nucleus of concupiscence remains in us after Baptism.
As long as he is on this earth man must always be on the *qui
vive* lest his passions flare up; hence the necessity for continuous vigilance over our senses and strict control of all our
actions. The admirable equilibrium which we see in the
lives of the saints is the fruit of victory won by long years of
heroic asceticism. Compunction establishes a supernatural
peace in the soul of the mortified man.

Christian penance plays another rôle of vast importance for
the whole mystical body: co-operation in the expiation of
the Redeemer. "Christ carried His Cross but He willed to
accept the help of Simon the Cyrenean; in like manner He has
appointed that a part of His sufferings should be undertaken
by His mystical body. This is the second reason for mortification: expiation, not merely for oneself, but for one's fellow
men. Seen from this point of view, the follies of the saints,
their thirst for immolation, is easy to understand."[68]

Dom Marmion gave first place to the mortification of our
state in life as being the most supernatural. "It is made up of
the burden of the day,[69] the monotony of life, the thousand
daily difficulties, and, for religious, absolute fidelity to the
Rule."[70] His counsels are always tempered by the discretion
characteristic of the Benedictine spirit. In preference to
extreme penances which tend to be a little ostentatious, he
prefers the mortifications common to all; illness and the petty

---

[65] Ibidem.   [68] Retreat, Maredret, November 1901.
[66] Gal. v, 24.   [69] Matt. xx, 10.
[67] Ibidem.   [70] Retreat, Maredret, November 1901

everyday annoyances.[71]   All these are sent us by Providence and mark out for each individual the true road to sanctity.

He does not condemn absolutely extraordinary means, but they may be the subject of illusion and must be the preserve of souls specially privileged.   "I am most eager that you understand my views on this subject.   When God invites a soul to practise them, extraordinary mortifications become a most precious instrument for its spiritual advancement, as for example, in the case of St. Mary Magdalen de Pazzi.   But extraordinary mortification is a gift of God, and just as it would be presumptuous to aspire to infused contemplation unless it were bestowed on one, so it would be presumptuous to adopt the practice of extraordinary mortification.   I have seen souls suffer great harm by embarking on these extraordinary mortifications without having been called to them.   Then God is not there to sustain us; nature takes her own course; we become ill and not infrequently the rest of our life is passed without mortification.   Christ has His own plan for each individual soul.   Do not worry if your superiors will not allow you to practise great mortifications; Christ will send you the ones which suit you best.   The Infinite Wisdom knows how to arrange it.   If we practise ordinary mortifications in union with the sufferings of Christ, they are of the highest value.   I firmly believe that these mortifications have a quasi-sacramental force to produce and maintain unction and fervour in souls; but we must realize clearly that our mortifications are of value only in so far as they are united to those of Christ."[72]

These are the chief effects of the virtue of penance which inspires, according to Dom Marmion, the spirit of compunction of which he treats at length when discussing the monastic virtues.   This detestation of the evil of which we have been guilty personally keeps alive in our souls that inflexible and salutary hatred of sin which is one of the most powerful forces in the spiritual life to preserve us from all evil.   This sentiment of contrition serves to expiate for sin; it consolidates us in our present state, preserves us from falling back into sin and introduces Christian ascetism into the radiance of the grace of Christ.   All Christian spirituality depends on the

[71] Ibidem.   [72] Retreat, Maredret, 1901.

mystery of the Cross. The *agendo contra* of St. Ignatius and the "path of nothingness" of St. John of the Cross are merely different ways of expressing the same necessity for death to self, which is an indispensable condition for a new life in Christ. As a true disciple of St. Paul, Dom Marmion takes, as the basis of his whole doctrine, absolute death to sin and a vigorous war against all the vicious tendencies of our nature. Like all the great spiritual writers he regarded mortification as being of no value in itself, but as a necessary ascetism for our fallen nature and moreover as being, in union with Christ, a means of expiation and redemption.

Life in God

The more one analyses the spiritual doctrine of Dom Marmion, the more clearly one sees the dominating part played by Christ in his teaching. His personal concept of a life of union with God was developed, not as a progressive practice of the virtues, but on the basis of a life centred on Christ. It took its form and its dynamism not so much from the systematic exposition of a St. Thomas as from the Pauline and biblical antithesis of death to sin followed by resurrection in Christ, which is the very essence of the Christian life.

Baptism is the spiritual symbol of this death and resurrection. "By baptism we are buried with Jesus Christ to die to sin and begin a new life with the risen Christ. If we are faithful to the grace of baptism, this death to sin and resurrection with Christ will become progressively more complete. A saint is a being dead to sin and participating in this glorious life with Jesus Christ."[73]

The Benedictine soul of Dom Marmion was profoundly struck by the Paschal Liturgy with its symbolism of the sacrament of Baptism. The splendour with which the ceremonies of Holy Saturday were carried out in his abbey, their symbolism, which evoked so vividly the mystery of death and life in every Christian vocation, renewed each year in his soul the appreciation of the sublime grandeur of our divine sonship and of the riches of the grace of adoption. His whole

[73] Retreat, Jupille, July 1907.

being exulted in it and his heart rose up in gratitude towards Christ who had saved him.

He likes to recall the many texts in which St. Paul discusses the splendours of this baptismal vocation. But his favourite text was that of the epistle to the Romans in which the Apostle expounds most forcibly the identification of the baptized soul with Christ, dying to sin with Him and rising with Him to a new life entirely dedicated to God. For it is "a death as a means to life, a mysterious power of substitution which enables us to reproduce in ourselves the thoughts, the viewpoint, the dispositions of the Son of God; which makes us, in a word, other Christs."[74]

Related thus to the mystery of Jesus, our Christian life appeared to him as an extension in us of His eternal Sonship. The doctrine of Dom Marmion, permeated as it was by the idea of the grace of adoption, could not fail to stress this aspect of the sacrament of our regeneration. His thought takes on a new grandeur when he touches this primary aspect of his spiritual doctrine: "Behold what manner of charity the Father hath bestowed upon us, that we should be called and should become the children of God."[75,76] And all the developments of his doctrine are introduced into the perspective of Baptism: "Every baptized soul puts on Christ. When the eternal Father looks on us He sees us in His Son. He recognizes in us the characteristics of His Son, and the more perfect our likeness to His Son, the greater is our union with Him, and the more are we the objects of the benevolence of the Father."[77]

Well versed as he was in the teaching of the Council of Trent, Dom Marmion realized to what an extent the life of Christ entered into souls regenerated by Baptism. He interpreted the formulas of St. Paul in the most realistic sense. The Christian "puts on Christ", that is to say he becomes truly "another Christ". The Head and the members are one. He declares it boldly: "On the day of our Baptism we have the right to present ourselves before the eternal Father and say to Him: '*Ego sum primogenitus tuus*,' 'I am thy first

[74] Retreat, Maredret, 1898.   [76] I John, iii, 1.
[75] Ibidem.   [77] Conference, Maredret, April 22nd, 1914.

born.'[78] We may speak to Him and act towards Him in the name of Christ. And God, seeing in us the characteristics of His Son, looks on us with benevolence. He is pleased with what we do, not for our own sake but for the sake of His Son."[79]

Risen with Christ, the Christian participates in the life of the Trinity. Dom Marmion did not fail to point out this fundamental aspect of our vocation in Baptism. While his personal inclination made him dwell especially on the Pauline thesis of death and life in Christ, as a theologian he was fully appreciative of the part played by the Most Holy Trinity in our baptismal grace. It is the Holy Trinty which makes us participators in the divine nature, which takes up its abode in the soul, bestows on us the three theological virtues and the gifts of the Holy Ghost, admitting us to intimate familiarity with the three Divine Persons. "Baptism contains the seed of all sanctity."[80]

His keen appreciation of Christ and the Church always directed the thought of Dom Marmion towards these, the most authentic sources of our Christian life. "I am often compelled by Our Lord to revive in myself the grace of my Baptism, my Confirmation and my Ordination."[81]

There are few authors whose spiritual teaching has been so firmly rooted in the doctrine of the sacraments.

Transformation into Christ

The Eucharist, which dominates the daily life of the Church militant, has a prominent place in the synthesis of Dom Marmion. He saw Holy Communion as the culminating point in our spiritual life. Nor could it be otherwise. The Eucharist is Christ present in person. As a young monk, Dom Marmion wrote in his private notes: "I see clearly that this sacrament is the principal source of grace. In it Jesus bestows on us, together with the Holy Ghost, all sorts of benefits and

---

[78] Gen. xxvii, 19.
[79] Conference, Maredret, March 4th, 1910.
[80] Letter to a Carmelite nun, Maredsous, May 9th, 1917.
[81] Letter to a Carmelite nun, St. Gerard, September 4th, 1918.

favours. I understand clearly that, if I could make my life a continuous preparation for Mass and an unceasing thanksgiving for it, I would receive at the time of the Holy Sacrifice an extraordinary degree of grace."[82]

There is perhaps no subject to which he returns more frequently, and it would be possible to compile from his teaching a magnificent opusculum of Eucharistic doctrine of which the Mass would be the crowning point. Guided by a deep appreciation of the Liturgy, his approach to this sacrament is always in accordance with its true, sacrificial perspective: "Holy Communion completes our union with Christ which has been begun by the offering of the Sacrifice."[83]

In full accord with the thought of the Fathers of the Church he saw in this presence of Christ among men an extension of the mystery of the Incarnation. He readily adopted the classic text of St. Thomas which affirms, in accordance with this tradition, that the Eucharist as a sacrament and a sacrifice applies to each individual all the benefits which the redemptive Incarnation has won for the world.[84] "The effects are the same as if one were present at the death of Christ on Calvary."[85]

Dom Marmion always considered the Eucharist as the very centre of all Christian life. Christ is there, wishing to communicate to us through the Sacred Host His divine life: "As I live by the Father, so he that eateth me the same shall live by me."[86]

While stressing the idea of efficient cause, he brings out also the idea of final cause in his interpretation of these words of Jesus. "*Vivo propter Patrem*. I receive my being, my life, everything from my Father; and because I receive everything from Him, I live only for Him. As you, likewise, receive everything from me, I wish that you live only for me."[87]

He often took this text of St. John and gave a profound

---

[82] *Private Notes*, Feast of the Sacred Heart, 1888.
[83] Retreat, Maredret, November 1901.
[84] *Sicut in mundum visibliter veniens, contulit mundo vitam gratiae . . . ita, in hominem sacramentaliter veniens . . . Et . . . effectum quem Passio Christi fecit in mundo, hoc sacramentum facit in homine.* III lxxix, 1.
[85] Sermon, Bouvignes, June 30th, 1897.
[86] John vi, 58.   [87] Retreat, Maredret, November 1901.

commentary on it from the spiritual point of view: "As the living Father hath sent me and I live by the Father so he that eateth me the same also shall live by me." To live thus by the life of Christ is the supreme perfection. Consider the sacred humanity of Christ, His soul, His heart, His will, all His energies taking root, as it were, in the divinity of the Word which proceeds from the Father. It is because all His faculties and all their actions proceed from this divinity that everything in Him is divine. In a certain sense Holy Communion should effect the same result in us: rooted in the divinity of Christ we should live by Christ as Christ lives by the Father."[88]

He appreciated the full value of the sacramental symbolism which presents to us in this "Bread of Life" the food of souls, and introduced it to good effect in his teaching when the occasion presented itself. "Christ instituted this sacrament under the form of bread and wine. He has said to us: 'My flesh is meat indeed and my blood is drink indeed'.[89] Being spiritual food, it sustains our strength, restores it, fills us with vigour and joy, making us capable of performing in a perfect manner all the actions of our life. When we receive Holy Communion the strength of our soul is revived. We have more courage, more generosity and more power to accomplish, for the greater glory of God, acts which are beyond our human possibilities."[90]

But leaving it to others to analyse in detail the effects of this spiritual food and following the deep-seated instinct of his soul, he goes straight to Christ, the source of life. Each sacrament brings us a special grace in accordance with the needs of our spiritual life. Baptism is the sacrament which incorporates us in Christ and makes us, by grace, what Christ is by nature, children of God. Confirmation makes us perfect Christians and soldiers of Christ, witnesses to God in the world, even to the point of martyrdom if needs be. The Eucharist effects our transformation into Christ.

It is on this central aspect that Dom Marmion concentrates in accordance with the general trend of his spirituality. He was greatly struck by a text of St. Thomas which finds an

---

[88] Retreat, Maredret, December 1905.   [90] Retreat, Maredret, 1905.
[89] John vi, 56.

echoing chord in his own interior aspirations, and he develops it with marvellous force. The holy doctor teaches that the formal effect of Holy Communion is to transform man into Christ by love: *transformatio hominis in Christum per amorem.*[91]

"The special effect of the Blessed Eucharist consists therefore in transforming us more and more completely into Christ. The soul which receives this sacrament with the proper dispositions is united to Christ and to His divinity to the point of losing its separate existence in Him. Through faith, the thoughts of Christ become its thoughts, through love, the desires of Christ become its desires, and by an act of perfect abandonment its will is entirely subordinated to the will of Christ. It effects so complete a transformation that the soul can say: 'I live now, not I, but Christ liveth in me.'[92] If I might coin the word I would say that the effect of the Eucharist is to 'Christify' us."[93]

Here again we are brought back to the fundamental concept of his spirituality: by Holy Communion we become another Christ. Christ leads us to the Father and our Holy Communion finds its culmination in the intimacy of the Blessed Trinity. "Jesus, the Second Person of the Blessed Trinity, is inseparable from the other divine Persons. 'Do you not believe that I am in the Father and the Father in me?'[94] When we receive Holy Communion we possess in our heart the undivided Trinity, the Father and the Holy Ghost being indissolubly united with the Son."[95]

"When, through the Humanity of Christ, we enter into communion with the Word, He bears us away beyond the veil of the Holy of Holies, *usque ad interiora velaminis,*[96] and brings us with Him to the bosom of the Father, *in sinu Patris.*[97] Then our perfect union with the Father, the Son and the Holy Ghost, with the undivided Trinity, is consummated, and at the same time—stupendous thought—our union with the whole mystical body of Christ; for 'Christ possesses

---

[91] Sentences iv, D.12, q.2, a.1.
[92] Gal. ii, 20.
[93] Conference, Maredret, 1916.
[94] John xiv, 10.
[95] Sermon, Bouvignes, June 30th, 1897.
[96] Heb. vi, 19.
[97] John i, 18.

a mystical body which is the Church, and our union with the humanity of Christ cannot exist without our being united with all His members. If we wish to be united to the sacred humanity of Jesus at the moment of Holy Communion, we must embrace in the same act of love Christ and all His members.' "[98]

The thought of Dom Marmion was never confined to the framework of an individualistic, introspective piety. It reached out to the vast horizons of the Church which are brought together in the sacrament of the Eucharist.

The other complementary aspects of his teaching on the Eucharist reveal the constant influence of his Christo-centrism.

The fundamental disposition of the soul which is about to receive Holy Communion is an ardent desire for union with Christ. "The Eucharist is above all the sacrament of union with Christ, *Sacramentum unionis*. What does 'union' mean? Being one with, *unum esse cum*. In order that union may exist between two persons it is necessary that the one finds nothing incompatible in the other. We must therefore abandon ourselves entirely to Christ so that He may identify Himself with us."[99]

The same spirit of union should inspire those divine minutes of thanksgiving. "The first attitude required of us is that of adoration. Christ is present in His immolation of love: we must prostrate ourselves before Him. We must not be troubled or surprised if we feel nothing: the Eucharist is the *mysterium fidei*, the mystery of faith. It is Christ's will that we often have no conscious appreciation of His presence, but only the conviction that what He has said is true and that He is there, really present in our soul. As Holy Communion is a mystery of faith it is often the will of Our Lord to leave us in faith alone. We should be convinced that God is present in this inner sanctuary of our soul, irrespective of our feelings, and we should ask Him to identify Himself with us."[100]

Realizing fully the needs of souls, the Abbot of Maredsous

[98] Sermon, Bouvignes, June 30th, 1897.
[99] Retreat, Maredret, 1905.
[100] Ibidem.

made a point of respecting their liberty in their relations with God. "It is best for each individual to follow the inspirations of the Holy Spirit. It is impossible to have a fixed rule. To try to fit Christ into our preconceived plan means hindering His operation and prejudicing our personal devotions.[101] You may prostrate yourselves at the feet of the Saviour and weep over your sins with Magdalen, or enter into the Sepulchre with Christ, or take refuge in His Sacred Heart. Likewise you may listen peacefully to the words of life uttered by the divine lips."[102]

Following the fundamental grace of his life, his own favourite attitude of mind was to lose himself in Jesus Christ and "to unite himself to the Word, to chant with Him the glory of the Father."[103] For him "the best thanksgiving is Jesus Christ Himself."[104]

Life of Union with Christ

The author of *Christ the Life of the Soul,* of *Christ in His Mysteries* and *Christ the Ideal of the Monk* is not a moralist giving a methodical dissertation on the different elements which go to make up our supernatural organism. It is not his object to consider each one of the virtues in all its ramifications in order to work out according to a scientific plan a complete code of conduct based on the virtues and the gifts. Nor does he seek to map out for souls the course of their ascent to God, marking the different stages of the journey. He does not follow the method of a St. Thomas nor yet of a St. John of the Cross. His special grace is to lead souls to Christ, to teach them to receive Him by faith, to identify themselves with Him by love and fidelity. Of what importance are their weaknesses, even their falls! Let them abandon themselves completely to Christ with invincible confidence in His merits and He will Himself lead them to His Father. There is a breath of real mysticism in this spirituality, with the splendid balance and upward urge of its Christo-centrism, carried away

---

[101] Ibidem.
[102] Retreat, Maredret, 1898.
[103] Ibidem.
[104] Ibidem.

with the Son towards the consummation of union "in the
bosom of the Father".

This contact with Christ is effected by faith. Dom Marmion
reverts frequently to the reflection of St. John on the coming
of the Word Incarnate among men: "Only those have received Him who believed in His name," *qui credunt in
nomine eius.*[105] This is a doctrine of capital importance
which shows the primary rôle played by faith in the foundations of our spiritual life. This, the first of the theological
virtues, is so essential that it was only by it that the apostles
were able to receive Christ as Son of God and Saviour. Our
adherence in faith effects even now in us this miraculous contact with Christ by which we become "His contemporaries".
We have no reason to envy the apostles and disciples of Jesus
who associated with Him in Galilee and Judea. "Why should
we murmur sadly: 'Ah, if I had only been privileged to see
Christ and live with Him, to hear His words, like the Blessed
Virgin, to serve the Saviour with the holy women, to lie at
His feet like Mary Magdalen, what progress I would have
made in sanctity!' After all, look at the Apostles. They had
spent three years in intimate companionship with the Master.
They had heard His discourses and witnessed His miracles,
but it must be admitted that at the end of these three years
they had not yet attained perfection. Why was this? One
reason is that God wished to show us by this fact that contact
with Christ through faith is more profitable to us than His
physical presence. 'Blessed are they that have not seen and
have believed.'[106] The less one sees, the more room there is
for the exercise of faith. We are therefore in the more favourable position. The more opportunities we have to increase
our merit in this way, the more profoundly does Christ operate
in our souls.[107] We enter into possession of Christ by faith.
The deeper this faith is, the more fully is Christ living in us,
the more fully does He communicate to us His Sonship and
all His virtues."[108]

Dom Marmion liked to recall the thought of St. Augustine:
"We approach God not by our feet but by our faith." *Propin-*

[105] John i, 12.   [107] Retreat, Maredret, 1905.
[106] John xx, 29.   [108] Ibidem.

quamus Salvatori, non passibus sed fide. "The stronger our faith, the nearer we are to Christ."[109]

It is not a theoretic or abstract faith that is required, but a living, concrete faith which casts us in adoration at the feet of the Son of God. This does not mean that Dom Marmion attached no importance to the intellectual adherence of our faith to the divine truth. His direction of numerous students and professors of the University of Louvain in the height of the modernist movement, his experience of contemplative souls and his relations with Protestants had given him an insight into the mystery of faith. We can see from his notes for his lectures with what rare discernment he had entered into the legitimate requirements of the human reason in its approach to the word of God. The vigorous intellect of the professor of Mont-César would have reacted strongly against any over-sentimental or anti-intellectual interpretation of his concept of faith. In him, however, the spiritual side was always dominant and the divine light which his soul received found its culmination always in an attitude of adoration in the presence of Christ. Instinctively his mind turned to the supreme truth which was the foundation of his life: "To believe is to abandon oneself to Jesus Christ."

His own personal faith drew him irresistibly towards this central mystery and, through Christ, he approached all the other truths of the Christian faith. "*Hoc est testimonium Dei . . . quoniam testificatus est de Filio Suo.*[110] This means that all revelation is contained in this testimony which God has given us, that Jesus is His Son. Our whole faith is comprised in the acceptance of this testimony of Almighty God. If we believe in the divinity of Jesus Christ, believe that He is truly the Son of God, by that very act of faith we accept the whole revelation of the Old Testament, which is realized in Jesus Christ, and also the revelation of the New Testament, for all the teaching of the Apostles and of the Church is summed up in the revelation of Jesus Christ. The man, therefore, who believes in the divinity of Christ accepts all that God has revealed. Jesus is *Verbum Incarnatum,* the Word Incarnate. Now the Word is the expression of all God's being

[109] Conference, Maredret, March 16th, 1910.   [110] I John v, 9.

H

and all His knowledge. The Word, by assuming our human nature, has revealed all things to us and by faith we accept all that He has told us. We can understand therefore that faith in Jesus Christ is the foundation of the spiritual life. There can be no other foundation than that which has been laid by God Himself: Christ Jesus."[111]

And thus we are brought back to the Pauline text which Dom Marmion used in almost every retreat that he gave up to the end of his life. He was profoundly convinced that all sanctity is based on Christ alone. In his eyes all the other truths of our faith are overshadowed by this paramount truth. It is the centre from which all the Christian mysteries radiate. "We become the adoptive children of God, we participate in the divine life if we believe that Jesus is the Son of God. To be born of God is to identify oneself with Jesus Christ by faith in His divinity. Our spiritual life will be more intense and we shall be more truly children of God in proportion as this belief becomes the pivot, the source, and the inspiration of all our activity. They are born of God and have conquered the world", as St. John affirms, "who believe that Jesus is the Son of God."[112, 113]

This faith in the divinity of Christ is the "basis of Christianity."[114] "Everything is comprised in it."[115] "The love and faith of the Christian soul should find constant expression in the one triumphant cry: 'Christ is the Son of God!' and give thereby immense glory to the Father. Such an act of faith would make our life an unceasing echo of that eternal act by which the Father engendered His Word, saying to Him: 'Thou art my Son; this day have I begotten Thee,' *Ego hodie genui te; Filius meus es tu.*[116] "By this proclamation of our faith that Jesus is the Son of God, we are in accord with the eternal Father."[117]

Such an active faith has its effect on our whole spiritual life; from it spring hope, love and the flowering of all the virtues and all the gifts of the Holy Ghost. But there is one

[111] Retreat, Maredret, December 1916.   [112] I John v, 4-5.
[113] Conference, Maredret, April 26th, 1911.
[114] Conference to priests, Louvain, about 1905.
[115] Retreat, Maredret, 1905.   [116] Ps. ii,—Acts xiii, 33—Heb. i, 5; v, 5.
[117] Conference, Maredret, May 9th, 1911.

effect which incorporates all the others: "This living faith surrenders us into the hands of Jesus Christ and establishes Him in our hearts."[118] "It fills us with the life and the virtues of Jesus Christ,"[119] until there is accomplished in us that programme of which the apostle was the living realization: the absolute replacement of our thoughts and sentiments by those of Jesus: "I live now not I, but Christ liveth in me." *Iam non ego, vivit vero Christus in me.*[120, 121]

It is not that the innate obscurities of the régime of faith have disappeared to give place to clear vision. Dom Marmion often stressed the two inseparable elements of our life of faith on earth: infallible certitude based on the veracity of God, and darkness, hesitation, even doubts. In his private correspondence we can often detect the echo of the aridity which he experienced at times in his personal faith, a faith, however, which remained unshaken. In times of the greatest darkness and vacillation he would redouble his fervour when he came to the Consecration of the Mass and, summing up all the vital forces of his soul, he would address Christ saying, with all the devotion of which was capable: *Tu es Christus Filius Dei vivi?* "Thou art Christ the Son of the Living God."

All the saints have experienced these arduous purifications of their life of faith. Dom Marmion's faith, in spite of violent and sudden "eclipses", was for the most part clear and peaceful and entirely unshaken. It was the faith of a mystic and of a Doctor.

We see no trace in him of those painful struggles of the converted unbeliever, no dramatic struggle against the faith. He was in firm possession of a truth which was his guide at all times, and by virtue of which he lived in the presence of Christ. He had no sensible perception of that presence. For most of the time he too had to travel by the way of pure faith, but the memory of the many lights he had received and his immense confidence in the word of Christ supported him when, like other saints, he had to advance towards God through the darkness.

---

[118] Conference to priests, Louvain, December 1905.
[119] Retreat to priests, Louvain, October 1898.
[120] Col. ii, 20.   [121] Conference to priests, Louvain, December 1905.

Even St. John of the Cross found his life of faith alternating between obscurity and illumination. If God gave to the contemplative souls in His Church for their instruction and consolation a Doctor of the calibre of St. John of the Cross to teach them to march towards God in blind faith, we must not forget that the saint of Carmel was the Doctor of light as well as the Doctor of the dark night of the soul. The final stage of the passive purification of the soul takes place in a night already streaked with the dawn of vision.

There have been great saints in the Church, such as St. Augustine and St. Thomas Aquinas, whose mission it was to show us another aspect of the spiritual life, an aspect no less essential, the luminous side of faith: *lumen fidei*. It is in this group that Dom Marmion takes his place.

"Faith is the splendid crown of our intellect, a light which enables us to cross the boundaries of the world of nature, supplementing the deficiencies of our intellect. Our horizon extends to embrace the infinite; by faith we enter into the secrets of God."[122] "It is faith which gives stability and unity to our spiritual life.[123] "When our soul is filled with faith, our whole life becomes a reflection of the life of God. For many Christians faith plays only a small part in their lives; nine out of ten of their actions proceed from principles which are purely natural. Their faith comes into play when they go to Church, and when they pray, but the rest of the time they live according to the lights of their natural intelligence."[124] Christ, for His part, lives entirely by the light of the Word.

"The child of God by adoption, full of faith, not only during prayer, but all day long, lives also under the eyes of God; he sees all things by a divine light, by the light of the goodness, the power and the providence of God. For him the whole universe speaks of God, the mountains, the sea, and all the wonders of nature. Everything speaks to him of God; he rejoices in the works of God; he rejoices in the works of his Father, and rejoices to see Him in His creation."[125]

Ascending to the plane of the eternal knowledge of the

[122] Retreat, Maredret, December 1916.   [123] Retreat, Maredret, 1898.
[124] Retreat, Maredret, December 1916.   [125] Ibidem.

Father, the exemplary cause of our knowledge of God by faith, he continues: "What is the constant object of the contemplation of the Father? His Word. The Father looks on His Son. He sees everything in Him. When the Word became flesh, He did not cease to be God nor did He cease to be a source of joy to the Father. The eternal Father knows His Son as no creature can ever know Him. Only He can fully appreciate the divine value of all that the Son does. In the eyes of the Father, the least actions of Jesus, a prayer or a sigh, assume an infinite value because they are the actions of His Son. If we had faith, our appreciation of the works of Jesus Christ and of His merits, of all that is in Him, would be unlimited. When we pray, 'our faith is wavering, like'· as St. James says, 'to the waves carried about by the wind.'[126] The trouble is that we cannot appreciate Jesus Christ as the eternal Father appreciates Him; we have not sufficient faith in His merits; we do not participate in the knowledge which God has of His Son.[127]

"A life of faith would establish us permanently in the divine life; we would see all things through the eyes of the Father.[128] We should live by God on earth in the light of faith just as the blessed in heaven do in the light of glory, present to God in Christ."[129]

The ardent faith of Dom Marmion inspired an unlimited confidence in Christ as our Redeemer. This confident reliance on Christ typified his personal concept of the Christian virtue of hope. While this theological virtue is based chiefly on belief in the mercy of God and His power to save us, in Dom Marmion it emphasized also the inexhaustible riches of the Redemption. At the thought of the infinite merits of the Saviour the soul of Dom Marmion exulted; his own wretchedness was of no importance; he was inspired by the same bold confidence as the great saints, and, in spite of being acutely conscious of his own frailty, he did not despair of attaining the highest perfection. He felt that he was the child of God and, in virtue of his grace of adoption, he made

[126] Jas. i, 6.   [127] Retreat, Maredret, December 1916.
[128] Conference, Maredret, September 1913.   [129] Retreat, Erdington, 1902.

bold to consider as his own the infinite plenitude of grace of the only begotten Son of God.

There was one text of the Apostle in particular which he often developed in a magnificent commentary, in which one could not fail to detect the note of personal experience. " St. Paul gloried in the fact that all he had was from Jesus Christ, that while immensely rich in Him, of himself he had nothing but weakness, infirmity and wretchedness. He felt that there were two men in him, the one poor and wretched, the other resplendent with the merits of Christ. So, when he comes to himself after his sublime ecstasy, he cries: ' for such a one —caught up to third heaven—I will glory, but for myself I will glory nothing but in my infirmities.' And he adds these astounding words: ' Gladly therefore will I glory in my infirmities.'[130] And why? ' That the power of Christ may dwell in me.' We also have our moments of temptation and discouragement. How miserable we feel at these times! We feel that we are worth nothing, that we can do nothing. Let us remind ourselves then, with St. Paul, that we are infinitely rich in Jesus Christ. *Libenter gloriabor in infirmitatibus meis.* If only we knew how to exploit our riches! We are so very rich in fact! In giving us His Son, God has ' with Him given us all things."[131, 132]

This unshakable conviction inspired a formula which became a part of him and which expressed his unbounded confidence in the privilege of compensation which all the members of the mystical body enjoyed in their Head: " Christ is our advocate."[133] We have only to identify ourselves with His infinite adoration and with the supreme efficacy of His merits.

This is the divine plan: " It is God's will to be glorified by the union of our weakness with the power of Christ."[134]

We have a revealing confidence made in one of the saddest hours of his life which unveils his fundamental attitude of soul in face of difficulties. After two years of absence owing to circumstances arising out of the war, he had managed to

---

[130] II Cor. xii, 9.   [131] Rom. viii, 32.   [132] Retreat, Maredret, 1898.
[133] Retreat to priests, Louvain, October 1898—Retreat to priests, Louvain, July 1902.   [134] Conference, Maredret, July 21st, 1916.

return to his abbey, and he was delighted to be able to visit
the community of Maredret and speak freely in this intimate
circle of all his inmost feelings: "I cannot tell you what peace
and joy it gives me to be back in my abbey. I am so glad to
find myself again in the midst of my children. Truly I had
not thought it possible to attain such happiness again on this
earth. . . . As you know, I have suffered a great deal in the
last two years. I have had many trials, but the thought which
remains in my mind after all these sufferings is that God wills
to be glorified by the union of our weakness with the infinite
strength of Christ. As the Word, Christ is the power and the
wisdom of God,[135] but side by side with this infinite strength,
or rather not side by side, but hypostatically united to this
power of God, there is the weakness of man. In order to
redeem us, the Word assumed the weakness of human nature,
as we have it in the text of the liturgy: *Deus qui pro salute
nostra, in assumptae carnis infirmitate. . . .*[136] *Qui in Filii
tui humilitate iacentem mundum erexisti.*[137] The whole
human existence of Christ is a revelation of this weakness.
Consider the infant child; consider Him above all in His
Passion: *Coepit pavere et taedere et maestus esse.*[138] We
see Him trembling, overcome with horror and exhaustion, but
still this union, this alliance between the divine strength and
human weakness gives glory to God. Hence that great cry
of St. Paul: *Libenter gloriabor in infirmitatibus meis ut
inhabitet in me virtus Christi.*[139] 'Gladly therefore will I
glory in my infirmities that the power of Christ may dwell in
me.' My strength is not my own, it is the strength of Christ:
'For when I am weak then am I powerful.'[140] That is the
one thought which has remained with me. Not that I had
not always believed it, but now it is graven so deeply on my
soul that it has become part of my very self. I am profoundly
convinced that I can do nothing without Jesus Christ, but that
with Him I can do all things. I experienced many sorrows
during this period: minor illnesses and weaknesses of all
kinds, and I realized more clearly that ever that I can do

---

[135] I Cor. i, 24.
[136] Collect of the Mass of the Flagellation.
[137] Collect of the Second Sunday after Easter.

[138] Matt. xxvi, 37.
[139] II Cor. xii, 9.
[140] II Cor. xii, 10.

nothing of myself, but that I must have unlimited confidence in this strength of Christ which dwells in me."[141, 142]

This two-fold realization which was impressed on the very depths of his being inspired in him some striking formulas which became veritable passports to life for many souls. "To realize our weakness and wretchedness knowing, however, that by the very fact of admitting them, we participate in the strength of Christ Himself, this is great wisdom and a great source of joy and confidence."[143] And in his final farewell to the nuns of Maredret, a few days before his death, he closed on this fundamental theme of his spiritual doctrine: "It is our wretchedness and our weakness which win us the strength of God."[144]

There is no form of Christian sanctity which does not find its culmination in love. This, the "first of the commandments",[145] is the soul of the Gospel, and the surest sign that we belong to Christ. But every saint has his own particular way of fulfilling this commandment and there can be nothing which gives us more understanding of a soul than the knowledge of his way of loving. St. Thérèse of Lisieux turned with all the enthusiasm of her soul to the Child Jesus and was heroically faithful in her resolution not to let slip any little occasion of sacrifice in order to give Him pleasure. The contemplative love of Elizabeth of the Holy Trinity enclosed her in the heaven of her own soul, not that she might enjoy the presence of "her Three Persons" as in the first phase of her spiritual life, but that she might chant there the glory of the Eternal One, nothing but the glory of the Eternal One, and thus realize, even in this world, her sublime vocation of "Praise of the Most Holy Trinity."

The theological life of Dom Marmion was dominated by the adorable figure of Christ. In Him he contemplated unceasingly the Word in all the splendour of His divinity and in the infinite grandeur of His divine Sonship, as the model and source of all sanctity, and the one way of salvation. Through all the stages of his spiritual life his constant effort was to

---

[141] II Cor. xii, 9.
[142] Conference, Maredret, May 21st, 1916.
[143] Conference, Maredret, December 1922.
[144] Ibidem.
[145] Matt. xxii, 38.

identify himself with Christ in order to enter with Him and in Him "into the bosom of the Father". He had only Christ in his heart and on his lips because it was Christ alone who reigned in the secret depths of his being. His soul was possessed by Christ. He lived in Him. He moved in Him. He worked only for Him. Every breath he drew, every act of love was for Him. Everything else, in his eyes, was value-less, unworthy of a moment's consideration. If at times his weakness led him to flinch under the weight of his heavy responsibilities, he would quickly lose himself anew in Christ and immediately his peace and confidence were restored. The whole history of his spiritual life, as we have said at length in a previous chapter, is summed up in this ever-increasing domination of Christ. It was at first the adolescent's devotion to his adored Master; later it became the burning passion of the young monk for his "One Friend, Jesus". The years passed, bringing with them a stable and ever-deepening friend-ship between Christ and him. At last, in the evening of his life, this union found its consummation in an identification with the Word in His love for the Father which was the realization of his ideal of sanctity: "I live now not I, but Christ liveth in me."[146]

Love, an ever-increasing love, strong and disinterested, was the secret of this sublime ascent.

Dom Marmion frequently found occasion to re-affirm the primary place of love in our spiritual life, as the principal means towards union with God and the measure of our acknowledgement of it. "We must try to be one of those souls who do everything from an active love. To work from a sense of duty is good, but to work for love is infinitely better. Love is the great way of making rapid progress, for it estab-lishes all the virtues in us and removes all obstacles to the divine action."[147] This love must be pure, free from all pre-occupation about self and directed primarily, not towards one's own personal perfection, but towards the glory of God, in order "to give Him the joy of contemplating in our soul a reflection of His own beauty."[148]

[146] Gal. ii, 20.   [147] Retreat, Maredret, 1905.
[148] Ibidem.

He insisted constantly and forcibly on the primacy of love.
He devoted whole conferences to it, and often quoted that
exquisite thought of St. Francis de Sales: "A trifle borne
with four ounces of love is worth more than martyrdom borne
with only one ounce."[149] He made his own also the celebrated
text of St. John of the Cross on the prodigious fruitfulness of
the silent and contemplative activity of the saints who have
attained the summits of the union of transformation: "One
act of love does more for the Church and for souls than a great
deal of exterior activity."[150] This is his own doctrine. "The
most striking actions, actions which draw on us the looks and
praise of everyone have value in the eyes of God only so far
as they are *in Deo facta*, that is to say performed in entire
dependence on Him and for love of Him."[151] He was fully
conscious of this truth: "At the close of our lives we shall be
judged on our love."[152]

As a great master of the spiritual life Dom Marmion had a
keen appreciation of the capital importance of love in the
Christian life. "Our hearts are made for love. We have an
immense need to love. The richer a nature is, the more
capable it is of great things, the more need it has of love. If we
do not love God with a great love, inevitably we shall come to
love creatures."[153]

These few quotations show how clearly the Abbot of Maredsous understood the deep-rooted instinct of the human heart.
No man can live without loving, and the whole problem of
sanctity consists in the right ordering of one's love.

Caring little for abstract considerations of psychological
analysis of the nature of love, he tried above all to present to
souls the various forms of love, the different degrees of it, the
importance of its rôle in the spiritual life, and the supreme
example of love, Christ. Dom Marmion was above all
practical: he was interested in the love which gave rise to the
practice of the virtues.

All this decided his choice between the two fundamental

[149] Conference to priests, Louvain, February, 1907.
[150] Letter to Sister Cecilia, Louvain, November 19th, 1902.
[151] Letter to Dom Idesbald, Louvain, April 22nd, 1906.
[152] St. John of the Cross.
[153] Conference to priests, Louvain, between 1904 and 1905.

concepts of Christian spirituality. In order to attain the
highest sanctity possible how should one begin? Shall it be
by a violent struggle against self, by renouncement, asceticism,
by the practice of humility and all the other Christian virtues
in order to develop perfect love in our souls? Or would it be
better to start from love and count on the irresistible force of
true love to purify the soul, to cure its imperfections and so
develop in it the practice of all the virtues? Dom Marmion
was quite definite in his preference for the second method:
"Love and do what you like," he used to say, adopting the
words of St. Augustine. He used to quote with a smile the
words of St. Francis de Sales when a nun spoke to him of her
plan of tending towards perfect love by way of humility: "For
my part," said the Saint, "I prefer to reach humility by way
of love."

He recognized, however, the advantages of both methods,
each of which had been practised by great saints. "Some
have devoted themselves particularly to the task of clearing the
ground by diligent labour, as for example St. Vincent de Paul.
Others, like St. Francis de Sales, achieved the development
of all the virtues by the practice and growth of love. This
is the shortest road to perfection and it is the one recommended by Jesus: 'This is the greatest and the first commandment.'[154] This does not mean that the other work is excluded;
but it is done for the love of God, in order to remove all
obstacles to the action of God on the soul."[155] Dom Marmion
deliberately casts his vote for the mystical method based on
the primacy of love; a method which is more in harmony with
the central idea of his own spiritual doctrine: "It is love
which distinguishes the child from the servant and it is love
which corresponds to our state as creatures. As the grace
of adoption raises our nature almost infinitely above its
natural level, so love raises and supernaturalizes our life,
giving it all its value."[156] How indeed could Christian
sanctity be anything else but love? "Is not the will the
dominant faculty in man? It is the will which sets all the
other faculties in motion. All conscious and deliberate

[154] Matt. xxii, 38.   [155] Conference to priests, Dinant, 1899.
[156] Conference to priests, Louvain, January 1902.

activity in man depends on his will; when the will devotes itself to any object, it devotes the whole man to that object. Now the fundamental and essential act by which the will devotes itself to anything is love. The man who loves God gives himself wholly to Him. The intensity and perfection of that love will be the measure of the perfection of his sanctity. That is why Christ, when asked about the nature of sanctity, replied: 'Thou shalt love the Lord thy God with thy whole heart and with thy whole soul and with thy whole mind. This is the greatest and the first commandment'."[157] And he concludes: "Love and sanctity are the same thing."[158]

The spiritual doctrine of Dom Marmion carefully avoided two possible exaggerations; on the one hand a meticulous and uninspired morality which would leave no place for the inspiration of the Holy Spirit, and on the other hand, a dangerous illuminism which would represent sanctity as consisting in fine mystical formulas, without any giving of self. For him, true sanctity implied the practice of all the virtues which constitute the web of the duties of our state in life.

"To be perfect a man should possess them all, but this is very rare: in one man austerity will predominate to the prejudice of gentleness; in another gentleness will overshadow fortitude, or fortitude kindness and so on. However, St Jeanne de Chantal used to say of St. Francis de Sales that one saw in him the perfect balance of all the virtues. He combined unshakable firmness with unchanging gentleness."[159]

There should be no juggling with words. From his experience of souls Dom Marmion knew that it was only the narrow path of the Gospel that led to the fulness of love.

When the Church wants to canonize a saint she begins by a meticulous examination of his virtues. Christian sanctity is a synthesis which requires a harmony of all the virtues under the dominating impulse of love. The example of Christ gives decisive confirmation of this point. We see the Son of God observing down to the last detail the least prescriptions of the law of God and doing all things well, *bene omnia*.[160] With His eyes fixed on the Father, Christ did everything for love.

[157] Matt. xxii, 37-38.   [159] Retreat, Maredret, 1905.
[158] Conference to priests, Dinant, 1899.   [160] Mark vii, 37.

In Sinu Patris

Dom Marmion was opposed to the over-introspective concept of the spiritual life which was liable to concentrate souls too much on themselves, preoccupied with a close analysis of their virtues and defects. He preferred the simplicity of the early Christians whose attitude was entirely different. For them, like St. Paul, Christ was their life: "*Mihi vivere Christus est.*[161] They had enthroned Christ in the centre of their hearts to be the source of their life."[162] In this way perfection is simplified. "It consists simply in losing oneself in Christ."[163]

To the soul which loses itself thus in Christ the face of the Father is soon unveiled and its spiritual life, in ever closer identification with that of Jesus, soon finds itself with Him *in sinu Patris*. There the union is consummated.[164]

Even when Dom Marmion borrows from other authors the thoughts which have struck him, he integrates them into his own synthesis. It was in this way that his spiritual doctrine, so simple and so traditional in itself, was gradually enriched from many sources. St. Paul was his most generous contributory, giving the force of cohesion to his Christo-centrism, but we have also the Joannine presentation of the life of intimate union of Jesus with His Father. This is really the culmination of his doctrine for, if the humanity of Christ is the way, the final end is intimate union with the Father. "It is the final intimacy of love which presupposes perfect love, confidence, and union of will. United to Jesus, we are *in sinu Patris*. This is the life of pure love which presupposes the effort to do at all times what is most agreeable to the Father. Our weakness and our miseries do not prevent us from being *in sinu Patris*, because it is the bosom of love and infinite mercy, but this requires a profound abasement and distrust of ourselves, all the greater because we are so close to the infinite sanctity. It presupposes also that we are leaning on Jesus, who "of God is made unto wisdom and justice and

---

[161] Phil. i, 21.   [162] Conference, Maredret, November 17th, 1909.
[163] Letter to the Abbess of Maredret, Louvain, May 11th, 1903.
[164] Conference, Maredret, June 26th, 1912.

sanctification and redemption.[165] Everything that is done in the bosom of the Father in the filial spirit of adoption is of immense value."[166]

Thus we may conclude our analysis of the vast synthesis of the Christian life as it was conceived by Dom Marmion. There can be nothing more simple or more sublime than this spiritual doctrine. We can feel in it the pure breath of the Gospel and of the primitive spirituality of the Church. We can perceive in it also the echo of that moving invitation which St. Ignatius of Antioch heard as he was going to his martyrdom: "There is a living water within me which murmurs to me from within: 'Come to the Father.'"[167]

[165] I Cor, i, 30.
[166] *Private Notes*, April 22nd, 1906, Sunday of Quasimodo.
[167] Rom. vii, 2.

III

THE PERFECTION OF THE CHRISTIAN LIFE

1. MONASTIC INSTITUTIONS

Fundamental Idea: The quest of God alone – The Abbot –
The Monastic Family

2. MONASTIC SPIRITUALITY

The Benedictine Ideal of Dom Marmion – Christ in the Rule
of St. Benedict – Conversion of Life – Compunction of heart –
Humility – The virtue of Obedience – The holocaust –
Fidelity through love – Fraternal charity – Contemplative
Prayer – The Opus Dei

Towards the highest evangelical perfection

THE PERFECTION OF THE
CHRISTIAN LIFE

III

THE PERFECTION OF THE
CHRISTIAN LIFE

HAVING established the fundamental principles of the Christian life in *Christ, the Life of the Soul*, Dom Marmion in *Christ the Ideal of the Monk*, showed that he was a master of the perfect life. He has the art of leading souls to the summits of divine love, and, a quality of infinite value which has won an immense influence for his teaching, he reveals to us, through the perspective of the Benedictine life, the essential and unalterable principles of all Christian perfection.

His fidelity to the spirit of the Gospels and to the teaching of St. Paul, his deep reverence for the Church and his single-minded devotion to Christ have given to his concept of the monastic ideal a note of catholicity which finds its response in all the religious orders and even among laymen. "Fundamentally there is only one religious life: Christianity: that is to say, the life of Christ in us. A religious is simply a Christian, *alter Christus*, who seeks the complete development of the life of Jesus Christ in himself."[1]

1. MONASTIC INSTITUTIONS

It is to the life of the founder that we must always look if we wish to grasp the fundamental spirit of an institution, and we find the explanation of Benedictine monasticism in the motive which impelled the young Benedict of Nursia, as he fled from Rome to solitude: God alone. Admittedly, in order

[1] Letter to a Carmelite, March 17th, 1914.

to have a complete concept of the Benedictine ideal we must take into consideration the Patriarch of Monte Cassino assembling around himself a monastic family, but nothing can give a better appreciation of the fundamental principles of Benedictine monasticism than the Sacro Specu of Subiaco. Personally, I shall never forget the impression made on me by this lonely rock from which the whole body of western monasticism came forth. Nothing can demonstrate more forcibly the immense importance of contemplative love than this naked rock which has become the source of an immense river of life which, still in our day, is flowing forth throughout the whole Church of God.

The fundamental idea
"The quest for God alone"

The Benedictine ideal has preserved, from its first days, the sense of the absolute and the eternal. When a postulant presents himself at the monastery, St. Benedict directs that he be asked this simple question: "Is he really seeking God?" This is the touchstone of his vocation. These words found their echo in the soul of Dom Marmion. For him also the monastic life meant leaving everything for God. All the rest was of secondary importance.[1] He had grasped the fundamental principle of St. Benedict with rare penetration: "There is a text of the holy rule which is always in my mind as the key, the essence, the very centre-point of all the teaching of our holy Father: *Si vere Deum quaerit.* These words include everything; the whole rule is contained in them."[2] "Whenever I give a retreat to priests or nuns of our Order, I stress particularly these words: Whether the soul is seeking God. It is for that alone that one comes to the monastery."

"A Benedictine abbey is not a university, nor an academy, nor yet a house for the formation of missionaries or preachers. It is a school of sanctity. If a postulant presented himself saying: 'I am entering here in order to become an artist or a

[1] Conference on the *Rule*, Louvain, before 1909.
[2] Conference, Maredret, March 4th, 1909.

scholar,' I would reply: 'Go to the academy or to the university.' Not that I do not esteem and admire the arts and sciences. There have always been artists and scholars in the monasteries of our Order. Our holy Father has said that we must use all the qualities that God has given us in His service, and the Abbot must foster these qualities, provided that there is no trace of pride or vanity in them and that they are exercised in obedience. But that is not the object of our Benedictine life. The one object of entering on our life is to seek God. If that is your object in coming, then I shall open wide to you the gates of the monastery and the gate of my heart. The quest for God—that is our one object. As our Holy Father has said, the abbey is a school of the service of God: *Dominici schola servitii* where we are taught, not human learning or art, but the service of Christ. The purpose of an abbey is to produce saints."[3] The genius of St. Benedict, or rather his providential mission, was to organize this single-minded search for God in the Church. Countless generations of men and women were to benefit by this new code of Christian perfection.

Before the time of St. Benedict, evangelical perfection found its ideal expression in the Church of Jerusalem, where the first Christians lived, with the apostles as their centre, detached from the world, with community of property, communication in the same breaking of bread, and sharing the same life of Jesus, forming "one heart and one soul in God".[4] This primitive community, modelled on the apostles, grouped around Christ, will always be the ideal type of every form of religious life in the Church.

We can see this gospel seed developing in full splendour in Egyptian monasticism under two characteristic aspects: the anchorite, and the cenobite, the eremitic life and the community life. The primitive form of Christian monasticism established about A.D. 305 at the inspiration of St. Anthony, was eremitic. There was no clearly defined Rule among the

[3] Conference, Maredret, June 24th, 1918.

[4] Acts iv, 32. Cf. *L'ideal monastique et la vie chrétienne des premiers jours,* by D. Germain Morin. Dom Marmion, who had attended this retreat (Pentecost 1891), had included in his private notes many passages from it by which he had been particularly impressed.

first anchorites, but extreme asceticism and feats of austerity and mortification which tested human endurance to the utmost, with all the dangers of a strictly solitary life which was uncontrolled, with no other guidance than the personal inspirations of these heroic men and women, who abandoned themselves to the guidance of the spirit of God, and sometimes also to the caprice of their imagination.

About the same time, the first monastery with a common life was founded in Upper Egypt by St. Pachomius, and the first monastic Rule was written by him about the year 315. There were several hundred monks in his monastery. He fixed a more or less moderate standard of observance, which was obligatory for all, leaving each one free to go beyond this minimum in his personal practice of asceticism. All the elements of community life were prescribed in detail: the office, private prayer, reading of the Scriptures, and work.

All the founders and reformers of Christian monasticism have found their inspiration in these two primitive types of Egyptian monasticism. St. Basil accepted fully this concept of the cenobitic life, which was the source of all the monasticism of eastern Europe. It was from his Rule, more than from any other, that St. Benedict took some of the basic principles of his own Rule. But these borrowings must not blind us to his striking fundamental originality. The Benedictine Rule bears the stamp of his creative genius. Man has need of guidance in his journey towards God. The eremetical life is a peak which, as a general rule, can only be attained after long years of discipline in the common life. "The anchorites are no longer in the first fervour of their religious life. Formed by a long period of trial in the monastery, they have learned, in the company of their brethren, to strive against the demon. Now, fully trained, they are ready to leave the ranks of their brethren, for the single combat of the desert."[5] Most men need the company of their brethren, and besides, it is by the constant exercise of the virtue of charity that the best men are able to maintain a high standard of perfection. These are "the cenobites, that is to say, those who live in community in a monastery and strive under the

[5] *Rule*, ch. 1.

guidance of a rule and an Abbot."[6] St. Benedict, with the spirit of a true Roman, organized this "strong race of cenobites", *coenobitarum fortissimum genus.* At their head he appointed an Abbot filling the rôle of chief, of shepherd, of doctor, and of father. Then we have the brethren, all united in the service of the Lord in the same monastic family, in which the *Opus Dei*, the divine praise, is always the principal work, and in which fraternal charity constitutes the soul of this common life established in stability and peace.

It is easy to understand how these multitudes of monks were raised by this way of obedience to the highest degree of perfection.

The Abbot

In the mind of St. Benedict the Abbot is the corner stone of the whole monastic institution. In accordance with the dominating idea of his spirit, he makes him the guide of the monks towards divine union, the father of God's family. Above all, he must imitate Christ in his position of shepherd: he must exercise every care, all his skill and all his tact, not to lose any of the flock whom God has entrusted to him; he must remember that he has been charged with the duty of guiding weak souls and not of exercising tyrannical authority over the strong. He must fear the warning of the prophet: "You killed that which was fat and the weak you have not strengthened."[7] The Abbot must rather follow the example of the good shepherd, leaving the ninety-nine on the mountain to go in search of the one stray sheep.[8] In the light of his own experience and under the divine guidance, which was in the nature of a revelation and well proportioned to his universal mission in the Church, St. Benedict was very careful to determine the function of the Abbot in the monastery (ch. 2.). Benedictine tradition has been unstinted in its admiration for this fundamental chapter which is perhaps the finest in the Rule. Princes and kings, heads of states, bishops and popes have sought inspiration from it in their control of men. Cardinal Mercier, one of the greatest figures of our times,

[6] Ibidem.　　　[7] Ezech. xxxiv, 2.　　　[8] *Rule*, ch. 27.

declared that he had never found any principles of government to rival those of the Rule of St. Benedict.

"The Abbot, who has been adjudged worthy to be put at the head of the monastery, must be ever mindful of the name he bears and justify by his actions his title of superior. In the eyes of faith he occupies in the monastery the place of Christ: *Christi enim agere vices in monasterio creditur.* Whence his name of Father, which is given to him as to the Lord Himself, according to the words of the apostle: 'You have received the spirit of adoption of sons, whereby we cry: Abba, Father.'"[9, 10]

The Abbot is, then, above all, the father of the monastic family of which he has assumed the charge and the responsibility: "He will exercise equal charity towards all; he will have the one rule of discipline for all, applied according to the merits of each individual. He must realize how difficult and laborious is the charge which he has received, to guide souls and to adapt himself to the characters of many. One must be led by gentleness, another by reproaches, a third by persuasion. The Abbot must therefore adapt himself to the dispositions and intelligence of each individual, so that he may not only preserve the flock entrusted to him from all loss, but also rejoice in its increase.

"Above all he must be careful not to neglect or underestimate the importance of the salvation of the souls which have been committed to his care, paying more attention to transitory and worldly matters. He must always remember that he has been entrusted with the task of forming souls, and that he will have to render an account of them. And so, for fear he may be too preoccupied with the material property of the monastery, he must remember that it is written: 'Seek ye therefore first the kingdom of God and His justice, and all these things shall be added unto you.'[11]

"He must wish to be of service rather than to dominate. He must be well versed in the divine law, preferring always mercy to justice, so that he may obtain a similar indulgence himself. Even when administering correction, he should act with prudence and avoid all excess, lest in seeking to remove too

[9] Rom. viii, 15.   [10] *Rule*, ch. 2.   [11] Matt. vi, 33.

thoroughly the rust, he may break the vessel. He must have ever before his eyes his own weakness and remember that he must not crush the bruised reed."[12]

No commentary is needed on these well-known pages. Their value has been established by the test of long experience, and the depth of thought contained in them speaks of itself. They constitute a perfect code of government in accordance with the institutions of the religious life in the Church.

So perfect an ideal of government does it present, says Dom Marmion, that not only doctors and saints but even some of the Councils of the Church have attributed it to the inspiration of the Holy Spirit. It is a striking fact that, through the centuries, a great number of Abbots guided by these principles, have governed large abbeys with great perfection. And even more remarkable is the fact that a considerable number of bishops and archbishops, including many canonized saints, have left their abbatial sees in the cloister to undertake the government of vast dioceses, to which they have brought glory by the wisdom of their administration and the sanctity of their lives.

Frequently in the course of his life, at Mont-César, at Maredsous, and in the general chapters, Dom Marmion had occasion to study closely these legislative texts. He read and commented on the Rule as a doctor of the spiritual life rather than as a jurist, and was able to link up his concept of Benedictine institutions and of the rôle of Abbot with a profound appreciation of the organization of the Church itself.

"The Order of St. Benedict," he said, "is a perfect image of the Church. Now, when Jesus wished to found His Church, He began by laying the foundation stone: *Tu es Petrus:* 'Thou art Peter, and upon this rock I will build my Church.' Similarly, following the example of Christ, St. Benedict has placed as the foundation of his monastic society a father and a leader who holds the powers of God Himself, and who is for his monks the incarnation of His divine authority and paternity. 'The Abbot takes the place of Christ Himself in the monastery': *Christi enim agere vices in monasterio*

[12] *Rule*, ch. 64.

creditur.[13]   This is the supreme principle which illuminates the whole spirit of the monastic life; but it can only be grasped in the light of faith: *creditur.*

"Chosen by his brethren and under delegation from God, the Abbot is clothed with a double personality: his personality as a man, marked often by many weaknesses and imperfections· and secondly, in virtue of his divine delegation, the personality of Christ Himself, of whom he is the official representative.   In the monastery it is the Abbot who fulfils all the functions of Christ: he is the good shepherd who leads his flocks to the pastures of life, the master to whom obedience and veneration are due, the doctor who teaches the divine law, the physician who heals wounds, the custodian of the House of God, and the pontiff who offers sacrifice and sanctifies, whose rôle as mediator achieves the consummation of all things in unity with God."[14]

The contemplative soul of Dom Marmion rejoiced in this sublime mission of the Abbot, taking the place of Christ, the priest, the doctor, and the shepherd.   There are excellent passages in *Christ the Ideal of the Monk*, which repay constant reading, in which he develops his broad supernatural concept of the Abbot according to the Rule of St. Benedict.   Some notes in his own handwriting, dating from 1918, reveal the deep appreciation of the rôle of Abbot, which he had acquired by virtue of study and experience.   On this subject, as on all others, we are struck by the vigorous Christo-centrism of his doctrine.   "As shepherd of souls, the Abbot shares in the dignity and the office of the eternal shepherd.   Now, the first duty of a shepherd is to feed his flock.   *Nonne greges a pastore pascuntur.*[15]   This food is 'the word that proceedeth from the mouth of God.'[16] 'The children of God live by faith which has its source in the word of God.'[17]   That is why the first quality which St. Benedict requires in his Abbot is to be in possession of this spiritual food: 'sound doctrine'.[18]   The wisdom of which St. Benedict speaks in his rule is a knowledge

---

[13] *Rule*, ch. 2.
[14] *Passim.*   Cf. monastic conferences, Louvain, before 1909; Conference, Maredsous, December 20th, 1916; *Notes*, 1918.
[15] Ezech. xxxiv, 2.   [16] Matt. iv, 4.   [17] Rom. x, 14.   [18] *Rule*, ch. 64.

of God and of holy things, drawn from the Scriptures· which
is inspired by the light of the Eternal Word and made fruitful by the Holy Spirit. This is the wisdom of which the
Holy Spirit speaks and which, he says, constitutes true prudence: *Scientia sanctorum prudentia.*[19] In a word, it is a
holy wisdom derived from prayer, which is assimilated and
lived by the Abbot and radiates from his heart like rays of
heavenly light and warmth, to bear fruit in the souls of his
monks. It is by this wisdom that the Abbot must form souls,
according to the model of Jesus Christ.

" The shepherd must not only feed his flock; he must also,
at the risk of his own life, defend it against its enemies. Now,
the greatest enemies of the flock are those who offer it poisoned
food. The Abbot must watch with unremitting care, lest
error or dangerous opinions should secure entry to the
monastery. That is why the Abbot must be, not merely pious,
but ' learned in the law of God ', *doctus in lege divina,*[20] so that
he may be able to recognize error, to condemn it, and to extir-
pate it without fear or human respect. That is why St. Benedict addresses these grave and solemn warnings to the Abbot:
' that he must never teach or establish or prescribe anything
outside the limits of divine precept. He must remember that
on the fearful day of judgement, he will be strictly examined
on his doctrine and on the orders he has given to his monks.'[21]

" Christ has said, ' I am the Truth.'[22] ' For this I came into
the world that I should give testimony to the truth.'[23] The
Abbot, who takes the place of Christ in the monastery, must
be a beacon of truth.

" Nothing can take the place of this living verbal teaching
of the Abbot. When Abbots neglected this primary duty,
when they permitted the poison of heresy and error to enter
their monasteries, as simony and investiture came in in the
middle ages, and Jansenism in the seventeenth century, it was
the signal for the decadence of the monastic order."[24]

In this age of modernism, it is good to hear such a vigorous
affirmation of the gravity of the responsibility for doctrine
imposed by the Church on those who have undertaken the

---

[19] Prov. ix, 10. [21] *Rule*, ch. 2. [23] John xviii, 37.
[20] *Rule*, ch. 64. [22] John xiv, 6. [24] *Private Notes*, 1918.

charge of souls. Dom Marmion was well equipped with this knowledge of things divine and it was in his capacity as teacher that the special grace of his abbatiate lay.

There is another aspect of the Abbot's function which, though not directly treated by St. Benedict, is revealed by the historical development of the Benedictine life and is stressed by the Church in our days in the ceremony of the blessing of the newly-elected Abbot: his rôle as pontiff. Dom Marmion appreciated fully this important aspect of his position. The Abbot takes the place of Christ. Now, Christ was the Supreme Pontiff as well as being the prince of pastors. It is this sublime ideal which the Abbot must imitate in his government. Pastor and pontiff, the Abbot shares this double rôle of Christ the Redeemer. As pontiff, the intermediary between men and God, it is by his hands that the gifts, the prayers and the homage of the people are presented to God. The pontiff must be pleasing to God, the friend of God, holy and pure so that he may approach God to plead the cause of the people. This sanctity is of primary importance, not only on account of the example which he offers to the people, but also on account of the vital radiation of the influence of the head on all the members. Christ was holy, infinitely holy, not only in His own person, but also as head of the Church, *Tu solus sanctus, Jesu Christe* (Gloria in excelsis). It has always been under the rule of holy Abbots that heroic virtues have flourished in the cloisters. During the solemn blessing of an Abbot, the bishop, laying his hand on the head of the Abbot, asks God to send down on him the spirit of His abundant blessing. From that moment the Abbot no longer lives for himself alone, or sanctifies himself for his own good alone. He lives for his community; he seeks to sanctify himself for the benefit of his children. He can say with the eternal Pontiff: "For them do I sanctify myself," *Et ego pro eis sanctifico meipsum.*[25] Every advance that he makes in the way of sanctity, each further degree of union between his soul and God, augments his power as pontiff before God, and makes his influence on his community more fruitful. On the day of his monastic profession he dedicated himself unreservedly to God

[25] John xvii, 19.

with a view to his personal sanctity; on the day that he is installed as Abbot, he dedicates himself to God in order to give Him glory by the sanctity of his monastic family, "that it may increase in merit and in number," *ut merito et numero populus tibi serviens augeatur.*[26]

"St. Gregory lays great stress on this function of mediator. He says that if an ambassador, instead of being *persona grata* with the sovereign, is unworthy and out of favour, far from advancing the cause which he is pleading, he is in danger of compromising it. It is not therefore solely on account of the example of sanctity which the Abbot, as pastor, should give to his flock, that his conduct must be above reproach, but also so that, as pontiff, he may be the friend of God, powerful in mediation and capable of appeasing His anger and making Him propitious to his monastic family."[27]

Thus, the monastery is the Church in miniature, with the Abbot, by delegation, taking the place of Christ.

The Monastic Family

It is by setting out so clearly the rôle of the Abbot that St. Benedict establishes the whole spirit of the monastic institution. He invites the monks as members of the monastic family to turn to the Abbot as to their father, and, in spite of his personal failings, to venerate him as the one who represents Christ in their midst. The soul of the monastic society, behind all its complicated organization, consists in this free and perfect submission to Christ, through the Abbot, and through Christ, to the will of the Father. It is a group-search for God under the guidance of a Rule and an Abbot, and inspired by a great spirit of unity and fraternal charity.

It is interesting to note the mutual respect which St. Benedict prescribes between the different members of the monastic family: "The brethren must obey, not only the Abbot, but each other in the conviction that, by this way of obedience, they are going straight to God. The orders of the Abbot and all the officers of the monastery appointed by him must come

[26] Prayer over the people, Tuesday in Passion week.
[27] *Private Notes*, 1918.

first; but outside of these the young monks must obey their elders with all charity and zeal."[28]

"The younger monks will show respect for their elders and the elders will have affection for the younger. When speaking of one another no one may call another by his name alone; the elders will call the younger, Brother, and the younger ones will call their elders by some term which expresses the reverence due to a father. As for the Abbot, because he is held to take the place of Christ, *quia vices Christi creditur agere*, he will be called 'Lord' and 'Father', on account of the honour and love due to Christ. When the brethren meet each other, the younger will bow to the elder. In this way they will accomplish what is written: 'Eager to give one another precedence.'"[29, 30]

These passages express admirably the atmosphere of respect, of cordial affection, and of fraternal charity which flourishes in the monastic family. The whole programme of life is impregnated with the supernatural spirit of faith, not only in the chapters on the divine office and the life of prayer, but even in the most minute details of the material life of the monastery.

Such is the framework and the spirit of the monastic institution, and it was in this atmosphere that the soul of Dom Marmion developed. He found in his Rule his living ideal of sanctity.

2. MONASTIC SPIRITUALITY

The monastic institution has its own spirit. Applying a general principle of religious psychology, Dom Marmion found that spirit in the model of the founder. Just as perfection for every christian consists in modelling himself on Christ, so "the Benedictine must be an imitation of Christ, but after the manner of St. Benedict".[1] The same divine plan included the Patriarch and all the members of his spiritual family. Hence that fundamental principle: "The

---

[28] *Rule*, ch. 71.
[29] Rom. xii, 10.
[30] *Rule*, ch. lxiii.
[1] Conference, Maredret, July 18th, 1917.

more clearly a religious resembles his founder, the better he realizes the divine plan ".[2] It was in this sublime light that Dom Marmion understood Benedictine perfection. St. Benedict received from God "a special grace as head of his whole family.[3] The more perfectly we reproduce the characteristics of our holy Father, the more perfectly we achieve our own sanctity."[4]

The Benedictine Ideal of Dom Marmion

There were, for Dom Marmion, two characteristics of the spirituality of St. Benedict: a great spirit of adoration and a great spirit of charity.

"As the ideal contemplative monk, St. Benedict was above all a man of God, *Vir Dei*. The rule is full of this spirit of adoration. When he is prescribing the celebration of the divine office, St. Benedict tells us that we should be "filled with respect and holy fear in the presence of the divinity."[5] We are to listen to the Holy Gospel, the Word of God, "with fear and reverence ".[6] At the Gloria all shall rise from their seats in honour and reverence to the Holy Trinity: *Omnes surgant ob honorem et reverentiam Sanctae Trinitatis.*[7] It is the idea of our holy Father that this spirit of adoration should possess us, not only during prayer, but through the whole course of our lives. 'The cellarer is to consider all the utensils of the monastery as he would the sacred vessels of the altar,'[8] and treat them with the same respect. 'The brethren must give one another precedence.'[9] On the arrival of guests, what is the first thing to be done? Welcome them joyfully? No. First of all 'let the head be bowed or the whole body prostrated on the ground and so let Christ be worshipped in them,' *Christus in eis adoretur.*[10] The mark of a Benedictine monastery is this spirit of adoration, not only at the time of prayer, but in all the details of life.

[2] Ibidem.
[3] Conference, Maredsous, March 20th, 1917.
[4] Conference, Maredret, July 18th, 1917.
[8] *Rule*, ch. 31. [9] *Rule*, ch. 72.

[5] *Rule*, ch. 19.
[6] *Rule*, ch. 11.
[7] *Rule*, ch. 9.
[10] *Rule* ch., 53.

"The second characteristic of St. Benedict is a spirit of great charity.

"Undoubtedly, the holy Patriarch wished his monks to live separated from the world, devoting themselves to prayer and the divine praise, but he appreciated that by becoming a monk a man did not cease to be a Christian and that the whole Christian life was based on the love of God and of one's neighbour. It was under the urge of this charity that we see him leave his beloved solitude to assume direction of undisciplined monks. It was the same spirit of charity that made him always ready to help those in need of his assistance in spite of his strong attachment to a life of recollection. He worked many miracles to help his neighbour in his spiritual and even in his material necessities. He was ever mindful of the fact that Christ Himself was not indifferent to corporal necessities and had twice multiplied the loaves to give food to the multitude who were following Him.

"It is his wish that all guests presenting themselves at the monastery be received. Some monks may, perhaps, say: 'We came to the monastery to escape from the world; if there is a constant flow of guests we shall still be in contact with it.' Our holy Father was careful to provide for this danger. It is forbidden to speak to the guests without permission, but he attaches great importance to the exercise of hospitality to those who come. A monastery which kept its gates closed to guests would not be a Benedictine monastery.

"Such then, is the true picture of St. Benedict: above all a man of God, a great adorer of God. That is why he directs that no work shall be preferred to the "work of God", *nihil operi Dei praeponatur*.[11] The divine praise is at all times the first duty of a monk. St. Benedict models himself on Christ who was, above all, the great adorer of the Father. But he does not forget that Christ was also the Saviour of men and gave for them the last drop of His blood. Though St. Benedict loved to live alone with God, as St. Gregory says: *In superni spectatoris oculis habitavit secum*;[12] yet the same great Pope tells us that he never hesitated to give up the joys of solitude to go to preach Christ: *Commorantem circumqua-*

[11] *Rule*, ch. 43.   [12] St. Gregory, Dialogues, ch. iii.

que multitudinem praedicatione continua ad fidem vocabat.[13]

"It was because of their full understanding of the spirit of our holy Father that so many famous monks, like St. Boniface, St. Augustine, St. Willibrord and many others evangelized whole peoples and won over to God nations in their entirety. It may be said that Gaul, Germany, England and indeed practically the whole of Europe was evangelized by the monks.

"In this domain too the spirit of our order must be appreciated. Religious congregations specially devoted to missionary work send out their apostles in search of souls. This is not our way. An abbey is founded where the monks chant the divine praise in choir and make the altar their centre. Before all else the divine Office must be assured. Then the monks can give themselves without reserve to the members of Christ's body while remaining within the limits laid down by obedience and the spirit of the Rule. In this way our Benedictine monasteries become focuses of sanctity, the heat and radiance of which reach out to souls."[14]

With this clearness of view and firmness of principle, especially in regard to the primacy of the divine Office in the Benedictine ideal, Dom Marmion combined a full understanding of the varied forms under which it had been realized in history. "Provided there is no compromise on essentials,"[15] he accepts sympathetically the most varied concepts of Benedictine monasticism. Like Christianity itself, Benedictinism is entirely catholic in its adaptability.

"Do we not see the most diverse aspirations manifesting themselves legitimately in the one Church of Christ: mental prayer, liturgical prayer, and the more active forms of the apostolate—all have their adherents. Some glorify God through the exercise of their arts and talents; others include even these in their sacrifice. And what is true of Christian society is true also of the monastic life. We cannot say of a monastery that it is not Benedictine because it consecrates itself exclusively to prayer. ' The Spirit breatheth where he

[13] St. Gregory, Dialogues, ch. viii.
[14] Conference, Maredret, July 18th, 1917.
[15] Conference, Maredret, July 15th, 1914.

will.'[16]　Another monastery may be inspired with an intense enthusiasm for missionary work.

"When I find a monastery with no exterior work, with no contact with the world, I have no fault to find with it.　On the contrary, that is excellent.　The Holy Ghost has inspired these souls with the desire for the essential without adding any exterior activity.　To others He may suggest the exercise of the ministry.　Provided that the monastic life does not suffer, the latter monks will be just as good as the former.　To question this would show a complete lack of understanding. We must have a certain broadness of mind and not be bounded by narrow ideas.　Just as there is room for every kind of service in Christian society, so also in monastic life.　Provided always that the essential is safeguarded, there is room for all schools of thought.　But if the essentials are not respected, then it is no longer the Benedictine life.　If we interfere with the essentials we are no longer sons of St. Benedict.　We may wear the scapular and the habit, but we are not Benedictines. A monastery may be as magnificent as you like; it may be built in the best style of Gothic architecture; if it is not organized on the lines laid down by our holy Father, it is not truly Benedictine.　The Benedictine life can only exist within the framework of the Benedictine system.

"However, once this essential condition is fulfilled, we can serve God by means of those qualities which He has given to us, in accordance with the different attractions with which we are inspired by the Holy Ghost.　The monks of Beuron do a good deal of ministerial work; that does not prevent their being very good Benedictines.　At Caldey they have no ministerial work, and want their monastery to be entirely contemplative.　I told them : 'That is very good; stick to that : it is the guidance of the Holy Spirit, provided you maintain what is essential to the Benedictine Order.' "[17]

Christ in the Rule of St. Benedict

We must always consider the teaching of Dom Marmion

[16] John iii, 8.　　[17] Conference, Maredret, July 15th, 1914.

against its monastic background. It was as a monk that Dom Marmion lived the Gospel of Christian perfection.

Now, the figure of Christ dominates the Rule of St. Benedict. When the postulant presents himself at his "school of the Lord's service", the patriarch of monks asks him only one thing: "Whether he truly seeks God"[18] and whether he is resolved to fight for the true King, Christ.[19] If so, let him enter the monastic army and advance towards perfection, "following the guidance of the Gospel and walking in the paths of Christ."[20] Let him not look back, but bear his cross valiantly, "sharing by his patience in the sufferings of Christ, that he may deserve also to be a partaker of His kingdom."[21]

On entering the monastery, he is received by the Abbot "who holds the place of Christ."[22] His life as a monk will be passed in this visible presence of Christ, for it is not in a man's presence but in that of Christ Himself, that he lives. In his Abbot he sees and loves Christ; he seeks only the glory of Christ.[23] It is Christ Himself whom he obeys with an obedience which is prompt, complete and joyous; for him "nothing is dearer than Christ."[24] He has only one desire: "to imitate Christ, who was obedient even unto death."[25]

Within the monastery he has found a family of brethren. Whatever their origin, rich or poor, freemen or slaves, they are one in Christ. They all bear the same arms in the service of Christ.[26]

In his daily life, according as he advances towards the final perfection, his actions are inspired solely by the love of Christ.[27] In accordance with the counsel of the Gospel, he has denied himself in order to follow Christ.[28] He is free with that sovereign liberty of the children of God. His one maxim is: "to prefer nothing to the love of Christ."[29] It matters little whether the bell is for the Office or for work. Like Jesus, he is entirely consecrated to the glory of the Father, and prays and works in constant union with Christ. In time of tempta-

[18] *Rule*, ch. 58.
[19] *Prologue*.
[20] *Prologue*.
[21] *Prologue*.
[22] *Rule*, ch. 63.
[23] *Rule*, ch. 63.
[24] *Rule*, ch. 5.
[25] *Rule*, ch. 7.
[26] *Rule*, ch. 2.
[27] *Rule*, ch. 7.
[28] *Rule*, ch. 4.
[29] *Rule*, ch. 4.

K

tion, without a moment's delay, "he dashes his evil thoughts on the rock of Christ,"[30] and emerges victorious.

He treats each of his brethren, and especially the sick, as he would Christ Himself.[31] He receives the guests who come to the monastery like Christ Himself. The poorer and more wretched they are, the more clearly does he see Christ in them.

Christ is the atmosphere which his soul breathes. In Christ he lives and in Christ he is to die. Sustained by the companionship of his brethren, he can realize his unique ideal: to love Christ, "to prefer nothing whatever to Christ, who will bring him together with his brethren to life everlasting."[32]

According to the teaching of St. Benedict the monastic life is a search for God,[33] following the guidance of the Gospel and walking in the paths of Christ.[34] Dom Marmion was familiar with all these texts. We come across them constantly in his private notes. His soul found constant support in them. For him Christ is the one great means of going to God.[35] "Everywhere in the Rule our holy Father places Christ before our eyes."[36]

The special grace of Dom Marmion was that this Christ ideal was the dominating influence in his life. He could not conceive monastic life, any more than the Christian life, apart from Christ. "As I have so often said to you, the Order of St. Benedict is simply the development in all its fulness of the Christian life. We are simply trying to practise as perfectly as possible what Christ teaches and prescribes; we want to live according to His precepts and counsels. Our life should be the perfect expression of the Gospel."[37]

The Conversion of Life

There are many ways of living the Gospel, which is the source of every form of Christian spirituality. Benedictine sanctity embodies one of the richest forms of this evangelical perfection.

[30] *Rule*, ch. 4.   [31] *Rule*, ch. 36.   [32] *Rule*, ch. 72.   [33] *Rule*, ch. 58.
[34] *Rule, Prologue.*   [35] Conference, Louvain, 1905.
[36] Conference, Louvain, 1909.   [37] Conference, Maredret, July 18th, 1917.

From the very beginning of the Rule, St. Benedict has been very definite in uniting his concept of the monastic ideal with the great movement of the return of all creatures towards God. It is a grandiose perspective which we find repeated later in St. Thomas and which gives to all forms of sanctity the character of a spontaneous "conversion" of man to God. Dom Marmion reminds us that, in order to have a full understanding of this thought, we must go back to the very beginning of the human race.

" God created man in a state of rectitude, justice, and perfect innocence. Adam and Eve, who were created immaculate, were raised, immediately after their creation, to the supernatural union. God bestowed on them sanctifying grace to divinize them and to unite them to Him. Their intelligence was illuminated by the divine light; their will was in full submission to the divine will; their souls were oriented towards Him; their hearts were filled with love of Him. The gift of integrity, incident to grace, extended even to their inferior faculties, making them entirely subordinate to their superior faculties, which in their turn were submissive to God. There was peace, perfect tranquillity, harmony. '*Pax omnium rerum, tranquillitas ordinis.*'[38]

" But, in the moment of trial, from weakness and self love, the first man preferred himself to God. He turned away from his Creator, drawing down in his fall the whole human race. Henceforth for all human beings, excepting Christ and Our Lady, sanctity had to take the form of a 'conversion', as we were all estranged from God.

" To remedy the effects of this fall, God sent us a second Adam. God constituted Christ the head of all mankind, the one efficient cause of their salvation, of grace, and of all the divine gifts. Having imitated Adam by our disobedience, we must return to God through Christ."[39]

Christ is the source of this "conversion", the foundation of all Christian sanctity. At the first moment of His existence, He turned towards His Father with His whole heart, with His whole soul, and with all His strength, establishing an infinite gulf between Himself and all that savoured of sin or imper-

[38] St. Augustine, *De Civitate Dei*, xix, 13.   [39] Retreat, Maredret, 1905.

fection. This is the perfection of sanctity: *Tu solus sanctus, Jesu Christe.* The Christian life consists in following Jesus Christ in this movement towards the Father.

Compunction of Heart

St. Benedict, who was accustomed to receive in his monasteries pagans recently converted, men of little culture and simple folk like the Goth of whom St. Gregory speaks, insisted on the importance of compunction of heart to stabilize the "convert" in the state of death to sin, and shelter him from any lapse. This, beyond all question, is one of the "dominant notes of the Rule".[40]

This may surprise us at first. Compunction is a word which does not ring pleasantly on the modern ear. It suggests an attitude of self-analysis, of dejection and sadness, calculated to stifle all impulse of enthusiasm and apostolic zeal. In fact, however, this profound appreciation of our state as sinners has its roots in the very essence of the Gospel. The ministry of Jesus began with the preaching of penance. The spirit of compunction is the very basis of all Christian spirituality; it is the normal sentiment of the "convert" and the guarantee of his perseverance. In this matter, and indeed in all the fundamental principles of the Rule, St. Benedict was simply reasserting the teaching of Christ.

It seems paradoxical that Dom Marmion, who was himself so jovial and spontaneous, could embody this aspect of the Gospel teaching. Yet this compunction of heart is one of the major themes in his spiritual doctrine. It is the custom in Benedictine monasteries to compose a eulogy of deceased Abbots and to read it each year in the refectory. The eulogy of Dom Marmion, which was composed immediately after his death by one of those in closest touch with him, Dom Bernard Capelle, Abbot of Mont-César, at Louvain, stresses this note of compunction as being one of the component parts of his Benedictine spirit. "Having entered the 'school of the service of God', by constant fidelity to a life of faith, humility, obedience and compunction, Dom Columba Marmion was

[40] Retreat to priests, Louvain, October 1898.

found worthy to penetrate the inmost depths of the mysteries
of Christ and to become familiar with that love which sur-
passes all knowledge, a love which was nourished by daily
meditation on the writings of St. Paul."

From the very first days of his introduction to the monastic
life, Dom Marmion was deeply conscious of the necessity for
this conversion of life. His private notes contain many entries
like the following: "I received to-day precious lights on
compunction and mortification, as well as on devotion to St.
Benedict and stability."[41]

"The angels veil their faces before the throne of God.
Filled with wonder and admiration at the sight of the infinite
sanctity of God, they proclaim aloud unceasingly: 'Holy!
Holy! Holy is the Lord!' As for us, poor sinners, still
journeying here below, the light of our faith arouses other
sentiments. As we contemplate inwardly the infinite sanctity
of the Lord, we must cry from the bottom of our hearts:
'Mercy! Mercy!' This must be our *Sanctus,* and the Church
has made its own this daily appeal: *Kyrie eleison!* 'Lord
have mercy on us.'"[42]

During the retreat preached by Dom Germain Morin, he
notes: "Compunction is the primary disposition of a real
monastic vocation." And immediately he makes the resolution: "While living in holy joy and even gaiety, to correct
and eradicate all trivialities and all dissipation, the sworn
enemies of compunction."[43]

Compunction of heart was to be one of his favourite themes
when preaching retreats. His teaching on this point was that
of a master. Starting, as was his custom, from the classic
texts of the Rule of St. Benedict, he developed it in the light
of the personal experience of a spiritual life centred on Christ.

Humility

The heroic ascent of the "convert" is pursued in an atmosphere of compunction and humility.

There is in the Rule of St. Benedict a fundamental chapter

---

[41] *Private Notes,* between April and June 1888.
[42] *Private Notes.*   [43] *Private Notes,* May 17th, 1891.

which Benedictine tradition has always regarded as the synthesis of monastic spirituality, and which contains, according
to Dom Marmion, the substance of his own concept of ascetic
and even mystical doctrine.

In this seventh chapter on the twelve degrees of humility
we have nothing systematic, but we are given a sober, vigorous
picture of the ideal monk in his search for God. As the basis
of his existence there is a clear appreciation of his wretchedness and nothingness in face of God; and in the presence of
His divine Majesty a filial fear which maintains in the soul
of His children by adoption a keen sense of the divine transcendence. This profound reverence before the infinite Being
is a characteristic attitude of Benedictine piety. There is no
trace of the dismal sentiment of terror in this holy fear of
God, inspired by love. The Benedictine soul feels that it is
the child of God. It longs to chant the praise of Him who
alone is existence itself. In comparison with Him who is
uncreated, all else is nothing.

"*Clamat,*" the Gospels proclaim it: "He who exalts himself shall be humbled and he who humbles himself shall be
exalted." This is the fundamental law which the holy
Patriarch recalls to his monks whom he seeks to lead to the
summit of humility and of heavenly glory. And he expounds
the twelve degrees, borrowed indeed for the most part from
Cassian but with quite a new spirit. The monk who assails
them with courage and perseverance will attain the supreme
heights of Christian perfection, where his life will be
stabilized in the pure love of God, "*mox ad caritatem Dei
perveniet.*"

Dom Marmion had meditated long and deeply on these
texts of sublime spirituality. As a young monk he had been
fascinated by them. As Prior of Louvain and later, as Abbot
of Maredsous, he frequently had occasion to comment on
them. "According to the teaching of St. Benedict," he used to
say, "the spiritual life is very simple. We have only to prepare
the ground, destroy sin, root up our vices, humble ourselves,
and God will do the rest. If we are perfectly humble, there
are no graces which God will deny us."[44]

[44] Conference, Louvain, before 1909.

God Bless You

Three words - but oh, how much they hold
Of loving thought, of earnest prayer;
Their value never can be told,
This triduum of words most fair:
        God bless you!

GOD!   Master of the earth and sky,
Omnipotent and All-Wise One,
Who guards us with a Father's Eye,
Who guides the stars and rules the sun:
        God bless you!

BLESS!   Love, caress, comfort your heart;
Sustain you in life's devious way;
His benedictions sweet impart
Upon your path from day to day:
        God bless you!

YOU!   Whom I would like to bless my
        friends,

But lack the power.   'Tis God alone
Can every gift and blessing send.
I beg before His Great White Throne:
        God bless you!

MY GOD, I know I have
THE STRENGTH OF SPIRIT
to accept the things I cannot
change —
I am sure I have **THE COURAGE**
to change the things I can —
I am positive I have THE **WISDOM**
to know the difference
**AND — YES, WITH YOU,
MY GOD,**
I am going to try my best to
use them.

FATHER WALTER E. JOHNSON
Maryknoll Missioner
SILVER ANNIVERSARY
June 13, 1953
June 13, 1978

Please Pray
For Priests

From the very beginning of his monastic life, Dom Marmion felt a special attraction for the virtue of humility: "I have received recently a light which seems to me very precious: God is contemplating me at this moment. He sees the depths of my wretchedness. He knows everything, even the contingent future. He knows clearly to what depths I would sink if He withdrew from me His grace. He knows exactly what I am capable of. For my part I can guess it from the experience of my own past, and indeed I would fall still lower, because the abuse of His grace would in itself be so grave that I would be led to commit the greatest crimes. This is strictly true every moment of my life even when I feel myself on fire with the desire to please God. I am so changeable! This thought humbles me and makes me to realize how good God is to sustain me, and to understand that I must put all my confidence in the merits of Jesus Christ. Humility, as St. Francis de Sales tells us, is simply the courage to face the full rigour of the truth in regard to oneself with all its consequences."[45]

Dom Columba studied the *Summa* and took careful note of the analyses of St. Thomas which go to the heart of the problem: "Humility considers submission in reference to God, and for this motive submits to his fellow men."[46] "Humility requires us to submit to our fellow men for God's sake."[47] "The humble man sees in himself only nothingness and sin. He can in all honesty put himself below his fellow man, whatever he may be, on account of the gifts of God which he reverences in him."[48]

As a true master of the spiritual life, Dom Marmion realized the fundamental importance of humility in the structure of perfection: "When we cease to progress in humility, we cease to advance in sanctity."[49] And he returns once more to the texts of St. Thomas which stress the primary rôle played by humility in the spiritual life in the elimination of pride, which is the greatest obstacle to sanctity: *Humilitas primum locum tenet in quantum scilicet expellit superbiam cui Deus resistet et praebet hominem subditum et paratum ad suscipi-*

[45] *Private Notes*, Retreat, May 1889.
[46] *Summa:* II-II, q. clxi, a.3.
[47] *Summa:* II-II, q. clxi, a.3, ad 1.
[48] *Summa:* II-II, q. clxi, a.6, ad 1.
[49] *Private Notes*, September 1895.

*endum influxum divinae gratiae, in quantum evacuat infla-
tionem superbiae.*[50, 51]

"God wants to raise us up, to make us gods. He has
destined us to enjoy His own beatitude, to contemplate His
ineffable essence, to associate with the Father, the Son and the
Holy Ghost, but it us by Him that this must be accomplished.
The sin of the fallen angels consisted not in their desire for
this sublime elevation, but in their desire to achieve it by
their own strength. This was a presumption which God
could not condone and Lucifer was cast down immediately to
Hell. The sin of Adam likewise consisted in desiring to
acquire by his own effort the knowledge of good and evil."[52]

"God is essentially the first cause. Our homage consists in
acknowledging Him as the source of all good: *Omne datum
optimum et omne donum perfectum desursum est descendens
a Patre luminum.*[53] The man who tries to act on his own
initiative is, in practice, denying this. Every creature is in a
state of complete dependence in relation to God. *Tota a Deo
et ad Deum.* Humility is the practical recognition of this relation. God has destined us to an elevation which is infinite
and which He alone can accomplish in us. Humility is the
habitual acceptance of this fact. The proud man is, more or
less unconsciously, putting himself in the place of God. In
his thoughts, in his words, in his actions, he is exalting himself, giving primacy of place to his own *ego*. Gradually he
begins to seek admiration and makes of himself the final end
and the centre of everything."[54]

The proud man seeks to take from God that which He
guards most jealously: His glory. And God cannot permit
any challenge to His glory. He cannot temporize with the
proud; they must be broken: *Deus superbis resistet.*[55, 56]

It was a joy to the Abbot of Maredsous to find in St. Benedict this grandiose concept of humility which places the soul
in the presence of God, and, in accordance with Benedictine

[50] II-II, q. clxi, a.5, ad 2.
[51] Conference to priests, Dinant, Epiphany, 1899.
[52] Retreat, Maredsous, September 1916.   [53] Jas. i, 17.
[54] Retreat, Erdington, December 1907.   [55] Jas. iv, 6.
[56] Conference to priests, Dinant, Epiphany, 1899.

tradition, he rightly regarded this chapter as the very essence of monastic sanctity.

"As the basis we have *Timor Domini*: a reverential filial fear, which maintains the soul in a constant state of adoration before God. Then the ascent towards perfection under the guidance and authority of the Abbot with the corresponding interior virtues of profound humility expressing the spirit of obedience, itself an expression of love and finding its culmination in the *Opus Dei*. Finally the goal, *caritas perfecta*, consummation in charity.

"When this stage is reached, a rule is no longer necessary; the spirit of God guides the soul by the inspiration of love."[57]

The Virtue of Obedience

Obedience holds a central place in the monastic life. It is an infallible guarantee of man's return to God through Christ. "As the human race had become estranged from God in the person of its chief, Adam, by his disobedience, it was the plan of the Eternal Wisdom to bring mankind back to God by the obedience of the second Adam with whom we associate ourselves by our own obedience. We have here the whole Christian life: to accept Jesus Christ and in Him the will of the Father."[58]

Dom Marmion admired this point of view, simple but profound, which raised by its theocentrism religious obedience to the dignity of perfect conformity to the will of God, and endowed the most trivial monastic activities with a great moral value. In this way it enabled men, within the framework of an ordinary existence, to attain a sublime life identified with that lived by Christ in the accomplishment of the will of the Father.

Modernism accuses religious obedience of constituting an abdication of the human personality, because it has not grasped the place which this virtue holds in the ensemble of divine rule. The Abbot of Maredsous had frequently to counter this new form of individualism and to recall firmly that submission to God through His representatives on earth

[57] Conference, Louvain, before 1909.   [58] *Private Notes*, January 1903.

was in accordance with the laws governing all creation. It is this indispensable hierarchy which ensures order and harmony in the universe. God governs men through men. This follows logically from the mystery of the Incarnation. But it is always God whom we are obeying.

Dom Marmion considered monastic obedience as "forming a part of the divine economy according to which God wishes to see all His creatures prostrated at the feet of Christ. It is a disposition of soul, in virtue of which man, for the love of God, is willing to prostrate himself before Christ in the person of the superior chosen by God Himself, whether that superior be sympathetic or not, whether he be perfect or imperfect. In my Abbot I must see Christ and submit myself entirely to Him. There is nothing more degrading to man than servile obedience. Therefore, in order that our obedience may be supernatural, we must see in all authority a participation in the authority of God: '*Non est potestas nisi a Deo.*'[59, 60] But this is only realized by virtue of a light from God; it is a question of faith. The greater your faith, the more clearly will you see Christ in your Abbot."[61]

Seen in this light, obedience attains a very high mystical value. Inspired by humility, it effects in a mysterious manner the substitution of Christ's personality for our own: "I live now, not I, but Christ liveth in me."[62]

As the emancipation of our real self, obedience becomes an infallible means of sanctity. It establishes us in the school of the saints, and Dom Marmion frequently reminded his monks of the unique strength of those great religious families in which, like the canonized saints, the members realized that they belonged to a veritable school of sanctity, *Schola Dominici servitii.* "The best monk in a monastery is the one to whom the Abbot can turn on any occasion, on whom he can impose any task, in the assurance that he will put at the disposal of his Abbot all that he has of talent and of physical strength, conforming his judgement and outlook to that of the superior. Such a monk is an unceasing sacrifice to the glory

[59] Rom. xiii, 1.   [60] Conference, Louvain, before 1909.
[61] Conference, Maredret, 1905.
[62] Conference, Maredsous, December 6th, 1916.

of God. Like Jesus he can say: 'I do always the things that please Him.' *Quae placita sunt ei, facio semper.*[63] His life is a canticle of love, like that of the Word Incarnate. Such a monk, even though he may be only moderately equipped for the work, will do great things for God and will be equal to every occasion; *loquetur victorias,*[64] for he will have at his service the divine omnipotence: *Voluntatem timentium se faciet.*[65] A monk who is perfectly obedient cannot fail to become a saint."[66]

The Holocaust

This quest for God by means of detachment from the world and abnegation finds its perfect expression in the monastic vows.

The monk leaves all things to give himself to God for ever. Religious profession effects a consecration of the whole being to God in union with Christ "in a holocaust of love".[67] Henceforth all his acts are clothed in the virtue of religion. His existence, like that of Christ, is entirely dedicated to the glory of the Father.

We would have an entirely false picture of religious perfection if we imagined that it consisted merely in the practice of fasts, abstinence, perpetual silence and other monastic observances. Religious sanctity consists in the perfection of love achieved through the perfection of sacrifice. The three vows of religion free a man from all created things and from himself, and enable him, as far as it is possible in this world, to make his life a constant practice of the virtue of charity. The soul lives for God alone, for the advancement of His glory and for the good of His Church.

Dom Marmion had a rare appreciation of the full import of the vows of religion and of all the monastic observances. He used to say that the practice of poverty "inculcated detachment from all creatures. It implies a high degree of the theological virtue of hope by which we desire God as our only true good. God is infinitely above all created riches.

---

[63] John viii, 29.   [64] Prov. xxi, 28.   [65] Ps. cxliv, 19.
[66] *Notes*, about 1901.   [67] Retreat, Dames Anglaises, Bruges, 1907.

The more we detach ourselves from all that is not God, the nearer we are to true poverty of spirit. In this way our vow of poverty becomes an act of homage to the divine Perfection. We renounce all created things in order to attach ourselves solely to God: it is a true holocaust."[68]

It is the same with the vow of chastity. Virginity is an acknowledgement of the supreme beauty of the Creator. The virgin soul knows no other desire than the desire for God: "My Lord, let there be no part of my heart which is not yours. I have no need of creatures. You alone suffice for me."[69]

Above all, the vow of obedience, which is the essence of the religious profession, completes this consecration of the whole being to the glory of God. Dom Marmion stresses this primary aspect of homage in the monastic vows by drawing a comparison with the more recent forms of religious life.

The modern Orders bring out admirably the social side of obedience and its primary importance in the service of the mystical body of Christ. It assigns to each individual his place in Christian society. Each of the different religious families has its appointed purpose and the individual enters with a view to a particular work. There are missionary orders, nursing and teaching congregations and a multitude of other congregations, admirably adapted to the multiple needs of the time and to the spreading of the Christian message. Religious obedience gives to each one his combat post and furnishes the Church with competent protagonists in every sphere. Dom Marmion fully appreciated this social importance of obedience: "It is not only useful for our personal perfection but it is of supreme importance for the good of the Church."[70]

However, his monastic concept of obedience led him to consider it above all in relation to God. "The modern tendency is to regard obedience, in the light of experience, as a necessity for the common life. St. Benedict makes it the vital and fundamental element of the monastic life. It is obedience which gives it its unity."[71] But even here we are

[68] Retreat, Maredret, December 1905.   [69] Ibidem.
[70] Retreat, Maredret, 1908.   [71] *Private Notes*, Retreat, May 1891.

only considering it from the point of view of utility for the individual. We must raise it to a higher plane: "it constitutes man's supreme homage to God."[72] "I became a monk in order to obey."[73] "We become monks simply in order to seek God, to render to Him all glory by means of the homage which is paid to Him by our submission. All the rest is merely accidental to the monastic life. But this homage is the greatest which man can address to God. Consider Christ. What was His first act on entering the world? An act of obedience: '*Ecce venio ut faciam, Deus, voluntatem tuam.*'"[74, 75]

Admittedly every form of religious obedience has God as its primary object but the monastic profession brings out more clearly this aspect of worship and of consecration to God. Monastic profession is made, not in the chapter room, but in the church or oratory during Mass. The chart is placed on the altar[76] to stress the symbolic union of the newly professed monk with Christ, Priest and Victim, in the same gesture of oblation to the glory of the Father: *una cum Christo hostia.*[77]

This concept of religious profession as an immolation and a permanent act of worship in union with Christ was a favourite theme of Dom Marmion. It was evident that he had made it the centre of his life. He used constantly to renew this formula of oblation during the Eucharistic sacrifice and at the XIIth Station in his daily Stations of the Cross. In his monastic retreats one of his favourite subjects was: "Victim with Christ by profession."

He held that all the sanctity of a monk was contained in embryo in his profession, just as it is for the Christian in his baptism. We have in it the same double aspect: death to sin and life in God, which is the essence of all sanctity. It only remains for the monk during the rest of his life to enter ever more deeply into this spirit of immolation and consecration which will bring him infallibly, if he is faithful to it, to the highest sanctity. "On his death-bed he will renew his mon-

[72] Retreat, Dames Anglaises, Bruges, 1907.
[73] Retreat to priests, Tournai, August 1922.
[74] Heb. x, 7.   [75] Conference, Louvain, before 1909.   [76] *Rule*, ch. 58.
[77] Cf. Retreat Maredsous, 1916; Retreat, Maredsous, September 1919; Retreat, Maredret, December 1921.

astic profession in an ecstasy of pure and perfect love before going to chant his praise before the throne of the Most Holy Trinity."[78]

Fidelity through Love

Dom Marmion had a special devotion to obedience, but he wished it to be an obedience springing from love. According to the word of St. Benedict, the monk practises an absolute obedience, *omni obedientia* but from the motive of love: *pro Dei amore.*[79] Monastic obedience always appeared to him as a free, joyous submission of the children of adoption to their heavenly Father and, as he liked to put it, "the complete expression of love."[80] He used to say that it was of capital importance to realize that Benedictine obedience was an obedience of love.[81]

The Abbot of Maredsous had always waged a vigorous war against one of the greatest dangers of the spiritual life: pharisaism. "In itself the Rule and all its material prescriptions are something altogether exterior and therefore accessory and secondary in the work of our sanctification. One could be perfect in exterior observance and yet be an unworthy monk. But obedience, though it is a small thing in relation to God, like all human things, acquires an almost infinite value if it is practised with love."[82]

"The object of the Old Testament was to guide the Chosen People towards Christ by obedience to the Law. In the New Testament everything is directed towards the interior life: 'The kingdom of God is within you.'[83] Exterior things are of value only in so far as they are expressions of our intimate dispositions of love for Christ and His Father."[84]

There are two ways of observing the rule: the one, a purely exterior and legal observance, the observance of the pharisee; the other, no less faithful, but inspired by love after the model

[78] Retreat, Maredsous, September 1900.
[79] *Rule*, ch. 7, third degree of humility.
[80] Conference, Louvain, before 1909.
[81] Retreat, Maredret, December 1916.
[82] Conference, Louvain, before 1909.
[83] Luke xvii, 21.   [84] Conference, Louvain, before 1909.

of the Virgin of Nazareth. Certainly nothing in the world would have persuaded Dom Marmion to disparage or belittle observance. It is by observance of the letter that the spirit is safeguarded. Christ Himself was faithful to the least detail of the law, but "our observance is of no value, except in so far as it is animated by the spirit of God."[85]

The teaching of the Abbot of Maredsous preserves a prudent balance between that laxity which is a fruitful source of decadence for religious communities, and rigid literalism which, by its exaggerated respect for the letter of the law, proves an obstacle to liberty of the Spirit. "An exact observance of the Holy Rule for the love of God leads infallibly to a heroic degree of sanctity."[86] He used often to cite the example of St. John Berchmans: "What did he do to become a saint? He simply observed his rule in the spirit of love."[87]

"It matters little if we are employed in the most menial duties, provided we carry them out in the spirit of love. We can do more for the Church in that way than a great preacher, because every act of pure love has its effect on the whole Church. It is like a flow of new blood which spreads through the whole mystical body of Christ."[88] This absolute unobtrusive fidelity is of immense value.

Fraternal Charity

Charity is the law of all Christian society and the soul of all community life. The rule of St. Benedict is a perfect code of fraternal charity. The monks must help each other to attain perfection. They must be animated in their relations with each other by a zeal inspired by charity in a spirit of mutual respect, bearing with the greatest patience one another's infirmities. They must have their hearts alive to the needs of the Church, ready to render service to all who appeal to them in the name of Christ. "I regard this point as being perhaps the most important in the whole spiritual life."[89] Nor is this surprising. St. Thérèse of Lisieux, who

[85] Ibidem.
[86] Conference, Louvain, before 1909.
[87] Retreat, Maredret, 1921.
[88] Conference, Louvain, before 1909.
[89] Retreat, Maredret, 1901.

had come to realize at the end of her life the full force of this precept of the Master, said something similar: "Fraternal charity is everything in this life."

Long experience had taught the Abbot of Maredsous the importance of this virtue in every form of Christian life. It is, he said, the barometer of the fervour of a community and of the sanctity of the individual soul. "I knew a religious who used to spend two hours a day in prayer; but if you went to ask him a favour, he would turn you down. What was he doing during his time of prayer? He was just turning over his own ideas. If he had been concentrating on God, the Lord would have taught him to give himself without reserve to his neighbour instead of holding back. The effect of his prayer should have been to make him see Christ in his brethren. It is only the souls who give themselves freely to their neighbour who really love Christ."[90]

Dom Marmion was fond of recalling the incident related by St. Jerome: "When St. John the Apostle was an old man he used constantly repeat to his disciples: 'Love each other.' And when they asked him why he went on repeating the same thing he replied in a manner worthy of the well-beloved disciple: 'It is the command of the Lord and it is all-sufficient.'"[91] "All the other commandments are presented to us as the precepts of the law, but this one is given us as the precept of the Lord Himself: *Hoc est praeceptum meum.* 'This is my commandment: that you love one another as I have loved you.'"[92, 93] And he quoted text after text, bringing together all the teaching of Our Lord on this one capital point. He regarded this new precept which commands us to love our neighbour as Christ loves us, *sicut dilexit nos*,[94] in spite of his natural deficiencies and all his infirmities, as constituting a sure proof that we belong to Christ. He asked for a pure, disinterested active love which forgets self in the service of others, and overcomes all natural repugnances to see Christ Himself in our neighbour: "Love each other in spite of the difficulties which you may encounter in the practice of this charity, and I shall ask My Father to fill you with the

[90] Retreat, Maredret, 1901.   [91] Retreat, Maredret, November 1905.
[92] John xv, 12.   [93] Retreat, Maredret, 1898.   [94] John xv, 12.

spirit of His Love so that you may become perfect in your charity and that there may remain in you no obstacles to the flowing of divine grace."[95]

And now he pictures the tremendous scene of the Last Judgement when, as the Master has told us, whatever we have done to the least among His children will be counted as having been done to Him: *Mihi fecistis.*[96]

It is a familiar doctrine, but Dom Marmion was able to give it a new force and vigour in the light of his Christo-centrism. "The true monk seeks to do good to everybody as though to Christ Himself."[97] "Those who have accepted the fact of the Incarnation know that God is present in their neighbour; if we do not love God under this form in which He presents Himself to us, we cannot love Him in His hidden sanctity."[98] "The Word Incarnate in His Humanity is incarnate also in His mystical body. We cannot dissociate the two. Our union with Christ is in proportion to our love for and our union with His mystical body."[99]

Dom Marmion was vigorous and at times humorous in his reaction to a certain type of mystical literature, which sought to reduce this fraternal charity to a vague spirit of affection for souls "in God". "NO." "We must love as God Himself loves. Now, the love of God is directed to each individual personally. He loves each one of us with our own individual characteristics. It can be said of every individual that there is no one quite like him. *Non est inventus similis illi.*[100] God does not love us merely in theory or in a general way; He loves each one of us individually as we would wish to be loved. A love "in globo" is not enough. So likewise, we must love our neighbour, not in an abstract general way, as if our brothers were so many heads of cabbage. True charity says: 'My God, I love you with my whole heart and I include in that love the sacred Humanity of Christ and, in Him, each of His members.'"[101]

"God embraces all the members of His Son in the one love. That is His great secret. Similarly if we are to receive fully

---

[95] Retreat, Maredret, December 1921.   [96] Matt. xxv, 40.
[97] Retreat, Maredsous, September 1919.   [98] Retreat, Maredret, 1901.
[99] Ibidem.   [100] Job i, 8; ii, 3.   [101] Retreat, Maredret, 1905.

of Christ our heart must be big enough to embrace the whole of the human race."[102] And the vision of Dom Marmion, like that of Christ Himself, finds its culmination in the longing "that all men may be one."[103]

Contemplative Prayer

A man of the spiritual calibre of Dom Marmion could not be insensible to the primary importance of prayer. He regarded it as "the strength of all the saints" and the secret of their "wonderful stability" in the midst of all the vicissitudes of their existence. "A child who clings to a rock when the tempest rages is more secure than the strongest man."[104] He himself invariably took refuge in prayer in times of difficulty. This vital communion with his God confirmed him in peace and gave him fresh heart. The attitude of a soul in prayer is the criterion of its life. Our sanctity may be measured by this intimate contact with God.

Grace and the other gifts of God penetrate the soul only through prayer. "I do not mean that prayer has objectively greater value than the holy Sacrifice of the Mass, the sacraments or the Divine Office. The Divine Office gives immense glory to God; the holy Sacrifice gives infinite praise to the Eternal Father in as much as we offer to Him His divine Son; and the sacraments are the channels appointed by God to communicate to us His grace. *In se* nothing can equal their efficacy. But in practice prayer remains the indispensable condition for the efficacy of all the other means. A soul who neglects mental prayer may recite the office, assist at Mass, and receive the sacraments; it will make little progress towards perfection. St. Alphonsus Ligouri, St. Teresa of Avila, and all the spiritual authors teach that our progress in charity depends on our mental prayer. The level of our mental prayer and the level of our state of soul are practically the same thing."

[102] Ibidem.   [103] John xvii, 23.
[104] Retreat to priests, Tournai, August 1922.

We must be careful not to confound methods of mental prayer with mental prayer itself. This problem troubled Dom Marmion before he entered the monastic life. " Many people think that mental prayer consists in making such and such acts, in going through a certain cycle, in carrying out the practices suggested by this or that book. Admittedly these methods may be useful, but we must not think that because we do not follow them we are not making mental prayer. There are a great number of people who think this, and I believed it myself for a long time. At the seminary we followed one of these methods; at the beginning of the book of meditations there were twenty pages or so explaining the use of it, and we thought that, if we did not follow all this, we were not making a proper meditation. I worked on these lines for years more or less faithfully and I found it all very difficult. It may have been meritorious, but I derived very little light from it. And, in fact, I have met priests who were convinced of the necessity of mental prayer and who had begun by practising it in this fashion, but had abandoned it altogether at the end of two or three years. It is important therefore to realize that prayer and a method of prayer are two quite different things."[105]

Does this mean that one ought to manage without any method? Dom Marmion did not think so. He knew too well from his experience of souls that beginners had to be led by stages to the divine union. He urged them to use the means adapted to their state. What he insisted on above all was the sovereign liberty which the soul must retain in its intimate relations with God. In this he is simply following the constant Benedictine tradition. The secret of the life of prayer consists above all else in letting oneself be guided by the Holy Spirit, and the Abbot of Maredsous never tired of repeating the advice of St. Francis Borgia: " the best method is the one in which one gets closest to God."[106]

It is for each individual to choose the method best suited to his own temperament and to his own needs.

" If you read the best writers on the life of prayer: St.

[105] Retreat, Maredret, February 1914.
[106] Retreat, Maredret, December 1916.

Teresa or St. John of the Cross, you will find this or that method described for making mental prayer and conversing with God. Some monks are tempted then to adopt this system, saying to themselves that this is what they must do. Now we must never forget that everyone has his own personality. There are no two of you exactly the same. And so it is for prayer: there are no two souls who have quite the same way of praying or talking with God. One can give, therefore, only a general outline of procedure in this matter of prayer. God adapts His approach to the individual character."[107]

The texts of Holy Scripture and especially of the Gospel furnish the ideal subject-matter for this life of prayer.

The first thing to be done is to fill your mind with the knowledge of God and Jesus Christ. In the beginning of our spiritual life we sometimes think that prayer comes of itself without any effort on our part. This is not so. God wants us to use the faculties He has given us. We may have to spend years learning to know God and Christ, becoming familiar with His words: *Verbum Christi habitet in vobis abundantur.*[108] We read in the Office of St. Cecilia: "This glorious virgin always carried near her heart the Gospel of Christ. Day and night, she never ceased to hold converse with God and to make mental prayer." If we wish to have a true, deep knowledge of God and of all that He has revealed to us in Jesus Christ we must study the Scriptures and meditate on them in our prayer. We must have the life and mysteries of Christ always before our eyes."[109]

It is the Gospel which has above all else the faculty of putting us in the presence of Jesus.

The Divine Office is a marvellous source of light for prayer and contemplation. When we go to choir, detached from all worldly affairs and recollected in the presence of God, we arrive almost unconsciously at a very high degree of contemplation.

Jesus often repeated the psalms when He spent the night in prayer, *Pernoctans in oratione Dei.*[110] A sublime prayer, ex-

[107] Conference, Maredret, May 9th, 1911.   [108] Coloss. iii, 16.
[109] Retreat, Maredret, December 1905.   [110] Luke vi, 12.

pressing the relations of the Word Incarnate with His Father!
If we recite the Office in this spirit, in union with the Word
Incarnate, we shall find in it a treasure-house of grace and of
light, a revelation of God to our souls.

The most important thing in mental prayer is not the
considerations, but the multiplication of acts of love. In
common with all the masters of the spiritual life, Dom Marmion stresses this vital point. " Our prayer must be a raising
of the heart rather than an exercise of the reason."[111] " In
prayer the essential point is to love."[112]

As an apostle of the doctrine of divine adoption, Dom
Marmion considers prayer as a " colloquy between the child
of God and his heavenly Father under the influence of the
gifts of the Holy Ghost, and in the spirit of an adopted son."[113]
The prototype of this life of prayer is to be found in the union
of the blessed, contemplating God face to face with an unchanging love. In this life it is "an intimate contact with
God in the shadows of faith."[114]

The Opus Dei

The ascending curve of monastic perfection is extremely
simple in its form. The Christian soul, being "converted"
and having entered the monastery, lives there in the contrite
memory of his sins, in compunction of heart, in humility, in
the practice of all the monastic virtues and in a spirit of perfect
renunciation of his own will, that is to say, in an absolute
obedience which is ready to attempt the impossible, and finds
its final expression in the formula of profession constantly
renewed. He lives there in union with Christ, a holocaust of
love.

Established by his vow of stability in a family environment
and in the atmosphere of fraternal charity proper to his
religious family, the monk devotes all his energies to God
alone, in a profound and unceasing prayer which finds ex-

[111] Retreat, Maredret, February 1914. [112] Letter to a Carmelite nun.
[113] Conference, Maredret, May 9th, 1911.
[114] Retreat, Maredret, December 1905.

pression in the formulas of the Liturgy at the hours of the Divine Office.

The Opus Dei is the culmination of the Benedictine life. It is there that the whole movement of monastic spirituality finds its accomplishment in the divine praise. From this lofty peak, on which the praise of God is chanted in an atmosphere of peace, immense benefits descend on the entire Church.

The discovery of the spiritual value of the Liturgy was one of the first effects of his monastic formation on the soul of Dom Marmion. He rejoiced in his Benedictine vocation on account of this office of praise which it was his privilege to offer to God in the name of the whole Church. " I am greatly helped in the recitation of the Office by the thought that I am the ambassador of the Church, authorized by her to offer my homage many times a day before the throne of the Most High."[115] The Liturgy was to remain at all times the central point of his spiritual life. He always regarded this vocation of praise as constituting, not the sole object, but the principal work and the essential mission of the Benedictine Order. " The Opus Dei is the heritage of our Order; we must value it above all else. We exist primarily to accomplish this work; it is our privilege to stand around the throne of God. Other orders may devote themselves to other activities, but we must put nothing before the Divine Office: *Nihil operi Dei praeponatur.*"

" Undoubtedly the whole human race is under an obligation to praise God, but there are many, even among Christians, who know no prayer other than the prayer of petition. There are too few who think of adoring, of thanking, of praising. Accordingly God has chosen a group of men whom He has entrusted with the accomplishment of His work, the Opus Dei. " There," as the Abbot of Maredsous used frequently tell his monks, " is the great work which God has entrusted to us, which He expects of us, for which He has drawn us aside. It is our function to sing the praises of God."

In the life of the monastery everything is subordinated to

---

[115] *Private Notes*, May 1st, 1887.

the Divine Office. We may devote ourselves to other works, as circumstances dictate, but the office is always the pre-eminent work.

This primacy of the Divine Office over all other monastic activities is explained by the importance of the virtue of religion in the Christian life: God is to be served first. This virtue regards directly the cult of God and compels us to give to Him the homage, glory, and honour which is His due. That is why the Church, as the interpreter of the divine will, imposes acts of this virtue on all Christians. She leaves them free to choose their occupations according to their aptitudes, but she insists on their assisting at Mass and receiving the sacraments. In a certain sense the Church may be interpreted as saying to all Christians: "Prefer nothing to the Opus Dei." This does not mean that the faithful are bound to devote most of their time to worship, but they must put worship and their duties of religion before everything else.

"As the monastic Order, in accordance with the thought of our Holy Father, constitutes a society in which it is sought to practise true Christianity in its perfection, it is easy to understand that it imposes the Opus Dei as the primary duty.[116]

"The Divine Office is called the Opus Dei because by its very nature it relates directly to God. In a certain sense every work might be called the work of God, in as much as it is inspired by the desire to please God. These other works, however, have no direct relation with God of their own nature; they only refer to Him on account of the intention of the doer, *fine operantis*. In themselves they are just ordinary activities. The Opus Dei is quite different. By its very nature, *fine operis*, it tends directly to the glory of God.

"As God is infinitely above His creatures, His work must be preferred to all else. That is why in the monastery, where we are bound to live the Christian life as perfectly as possible, everything centres round the Opus Dei. Before the sixteenth century there were no religious orders which did not recite the Office in choir. Nowadays there are congregations in which the religious recite the Office in private. They have

116 *Rule*, ch. 43.

been formed for a special purpose. In other congregations, while the Office is recited in common, it is only of secondary importance in the disposition of the day. They try to arrange the recitation of the Hours so as not to interfere with the works to which their institute is dedicated.

"It is not so with us. The best hours of the day are given to the Office: it is our principal work, not only from the importance we attach to it, but also in practice by the place which we reserve for it in the order of our day. The Benedictines have always regarded the Divine Office as the principal work of their life, so that any occupations which interfere with it cannot be admitted. That is why our Holy Father says: *Nihil Operi Dei praeponatur.* 'Let nothing be preferred to the Divine Office'[117]: nothing—neither reading, nor work—absolutely nothing."

The excellence of the Divine Office is derived from its very nature; it is the canticle of the Word prolonged in the praise of the Church. "As the Word, Jesus is the glory of His Father, 'the brightness of His glory and the figure of His substance', His subsisting, essential, infinite, ineffable glory: *Splendor gloriae et figura substantiae eius.*[118] The Word is the Canticle which the Father chants eternally and which is for Him an infinite source of glory. That is why the glory of God is as unfathomable as God Himself. In Heaven we shall understand that the *Verbum*, by this Word, which is Himself, gives infinite praise to the Father.

"Through the Divine Office we associate ourselves with the Word. The Church and He are one. The Office is the voice of the Spouse, united to Christ in this work of the glorification of the Father." This is a sublime concept corresponding to the noble idea of Pius XII who sees in the Liturgy the exercise of the priesthood of Christ perpetuated in His Church.

The Church is the complement of Christ; in her and through her the work of the Redemption is continued in all its aspects; apostolic activity, suffering as a means of expiation and redemption, prayer, and praise. Christ continues to glorify His Father through the voice of His Church, *vox Sponsae.*

[117] *Rule*, ch. 43.   [118] Heb. i, 3.

Thus the whole movement of Benedictine spirituality takes place in the life of the Church. Every religious institution is an expression of one of the aspects of the mystery of Christ: the monk consecrates his whole life to the single-minded quest for God and, when he has found Him, he sings His praises.

IV

SACERDOS ALTER CHRISTUS

1. CHRIST A PRIEST FOR EVER

The prototype of the priesthood in the Trinity – The consecration of Christ as a Priest – The "Ecce venio" – The sacrifice of the Cross – The sacrifice of the altar – The Eternal Priesthood

2. THE PRIESTHOOD IN THE CHURCH

Grandeur of the priest – Priestly sanctity – Fundamental principle: "Sacerdos alter Christus – Eminent sanctity of the priest – Spirit of faith – Virtue of religion – the Mass of the priest – Spirit of prayer – the other priestly virtues

The Priest is another Christ

IV

SACERDOS ALTER CHRISTUS[1]

HAVING been dedicated to the priesthood from his youth, and having undergone long years of formation first at the seminary in Clonliffe, then at the Propaganda College in Rome, Dom Marmion had devoted five years to the ministry and to teaching in the diocese of Dublin, and these experiences had left their mark on him. He retained a deep understanding of the grandeur of the priesthood. He was always at his ease and, as it were, in his element, among the many priests whom he used to meet. His own spirit was essentially priestly. As a monk, the Mass continued to be the centre of his life. In face of the problems of his time, his reaction was always that of a priest. Although less preoccupied than we are with the strictly pastoral function of the priesthood, his deep feeling for the Church revealed him as being ever the priest at the service of souls and conscious of his sublime vocation as a mediator. The recent publication of *Christ, the Ideal of the Priest* shows him to us a master of priestly spirituality.

Admittedly his synthesis is not complete, but that is not to be wondered at. Even now the theology of the priesthood is only being built up. To appreciate the gradual development by the Church herself of these great questions we have only to compare the successive pontifical pronouncements reflecting in their directions the contemporary preoccupations. The masterly encyclical of Pius XI on the Catholic priesthood hardly mentions the pastoral responsibility of the priest to which a large part of the more recent exhortation of Pius XII is devoted. The teaching of Pius XI is, none the less, rich in doctrine and still vital to-day.

[1] Title intended by Dom Marmion. Cf. Letter, March 6th, 1918.

The same may be said of the teaching of Dom Marmion on the priesthood. A priest who is deeply involved in the contemporary movement testified to his worth as follows: " Certainly the man who regards pastoral theology as being simply a collection of ready-made recipes will be disappointed in Dom Marmion. He has, as always, gone straight to the essentials: the Gospels and St. Paul. The soul who studies his teaching finds itself bathed in an atmsophere which is essentially supernatural while at the same time it is brought face to face with what the service of the Lord demands of it: to leave all things and follow Him. It is raised to a plane which is far above all considerations of human success and all deception, the plane of pure faith, of abandonment to the Father through the Son, of submissiveness to the Holy Spirit and fidelity to the Church. Such a soul finds itself well prepared, ready at any moment to respond to the impulse of grace. He may be a lay apostle, a curate in the suburbs, a country parish priest; he may be a monk or a missionary; it makes no difference; he will be a strong instrument in the hands of Christ for the furtherance of His kingdom."[2]

If Dom Marmion does not furnish an immediate solution for all the problems which face us to-day, he indicates clearly the lines which we should follow. He has brought out clearly the unchanging values of the priesthood and for that reason his doctrine, like his spirituality, can never be out of date.

1. CHRIST, A PRIEST FOR EVER

In the concept of Dom Marmion, the priesthood is the culmination of our identification with Christ. If the ordinary Christian or monk finds in Christ his ideal model, how much more should this be so for the priest, whose sublime mission it is to live on this earth as another Christ.

The Prototype of the Priesthood in the Trinity

The Benedictine theologian sees in the mystery of the most

[2] Pierre Jounel in *Présence de Dom Marmion*, pp. 178-185.

holy Trinity the supreme exemplar of the priesthood of Christ. At first sight this concept seems surprising, but Dom Marmion, ever scrupulous for doctrinal exactitude, does not fail to elaborate his idea, and his exposition of the priesthood is enhanced by the profound wisdom of this viewpoint. Admittedly—and the Abbot of Maredsous is careful to insist on this point—the priesthood is an exclusive attribute of the sacred Humanity of Jesus, implying, as it does, adoration and other acts of religion which would be incompatible for God, as God. Still we may see in God the prototype of the priesthood. How is this? I shall explain. God, in His essence, is great and infinitely worthy of praise: *magnus et laudabilis nimis.*[1] It is necessary, therefore, that God should receive what is due to this grandeur and to this dignity. It is fitting that God should be praised for what He is in Himself, and for all that He creates, if it is His will to create. God could have remained in the sacrosanct isolation of the most holy Trinity. In it lies hidden an infinite life, the reciprocal donation of the divine Persons in mutual love. The three Persons constitute the intimate life and joy of God. He has need of nothing outside of Himself.

"Now, if we consider the three divine Persons and their mutual relations we see there the prototype of the priesthood. You are familiar with the etymology of the word 'sacerdos': *sacra dans.* The Son receives from the Father the gift which is supremely sacred, the gift of the life of the Father Himself. The Father, in fact, by engendering Him, communicates to Him His nature, His life, His perfection, His beatitude, all that He is, except His Fatherhood. The Son by reciprocation gives to the Father in a transport of infinite love all that He receives of Him except His Sonship. From this mutual donation proceeds the Holy Ghost, who receives everything from the Father and the Son and who, by a movement of infinite love, returns to the Father and the Son all that He receives from Them. It is in this ineffable donation which the divine Persons make to each other in the bosom of the most holy Trinity that we can see the prototype of the priesthood. There can be no question here certainly of adoration, of immola-

[1] Ps. xlviii, 2 and cxliv, 3.

tion or of those other acts which are the constituent elements of the priesthood in the strict sense, because, as between the divine Persons, there is neither superiority nor inferiority; but we can see there the transcendent prototype of the priesthood because everything that is created exists in God supereminently."

This is sound doctrine. It casts a new light on all the theology of the priesthood of the Word Incarnate. There is no confusion in the thought of the Abbot of Maredsous. In his expositions he has recourse to scholastic distinctions which bring out exactly the sense and the scope of this sublime concept which had long been familiar to him. " The priesthood of Christ is a consequence of the mystery of the Incarnation, but in order to understand all that it involves we must enter into the mystery of the holy and adorable Trinity. The second Person of the Trinity, the Word, renders to the Father a glory which is infinite. He is His essential glory: *splendor gloriae et figura substantiae.*[2] As the Word, before His Incarnation, He did not offer to the Father sacrifice in the strict sense because sacrifice supposes adoration, an admission of inferiority in relation to Him who is adored; it is a recognition of His grandeur by one's own abasement. The Word, being equal to the Father, being one with Him, could not offer Him sacrifice, strictly speaking, *formaliter*, but He procured for Him *eminenter* all the glory which is derived from sacrifice."

Dom Marmion's conclusion is unequivocal: " In the strict sense the priesthood is not in God. As the Word, Christ could not be priest."

The Consecration of Christ as Priest

For a full understanding of the priesthood of the Word Incarnate we must go to Nazareth to assist at that sublime scene when God brought about at the same time the divine maternity of Mary and the consecration of her Son as Priest. Dom Marmion liked to meditate on this decisive moment in the

[2] Heb. i, 3.

history of the world which gave us, in the words of St. Paul, the Son of God Himself as High Priest: Habemus Pontificem . . . Filium Dei,[3] a God-Priest, but priest by virtue of His human nature, which He assumed in the womb of the Virgin Mary on the day of His Incarnation.

When the angel announced to Mary that she was to become the Mother of God, when he said to her, "The Holy Ghost shall come upon thee and the power of the Most High shall overshadow thee. And therefore also He who shall be born of thee shall be called the Son of God,"[4] the Virgin replied: "Behold the handmaid of the Lord; be it done to me according to thy word." Then the Word was made flesh, and at the same moment the first priest was consecrated, and a cry was heard from heaven: "Thou art a Priest for ever." A priest by divine vocation, for "Christ did not glorify Himself that He might be made a high priest but He that said unto Him: 'Thou art my Son, this day have I begotten Thee. Thou art a priest for ever according to the order of Melchisedech."[5, 6]

This priesthood of the Word is in Christ, in His quality as man, as is made clear in the Epistle to the Hebrews: "taken from among men"; but it derives its origin, its sublime grandeur, and its omnipotent efficacy from the fact that it is rooted in the hypostatic union. The Incarnation accomplished in Christ the union of the two natures in the person of the Word. "In virtue of one of these natures He could say: 'I and the Father are one';[7] in virtue of the other: 'The Father is greater than I.'[8] It was as Man-God that Christ was able to offer sacrifice to His Father."[9]

Dom Marmion was familiar with the classical doctrine on the nature of the priesthood of Christ, finding its ultimate basis in the hypostatic union which gave an infinite value to the smallest personal actions of the Man-God. He did not seek to establish in a learned dissertation the fundamental essence of the priesthood; his aim was to examine its

---

[3] Heb. iv, 14.　　　[6] Conference, Maredret, July 8th, 1914.
[4] Luke i, 35.　　　[7] John x, 30.
[5] Heb. v, 5-6.　　　[8] John xiv, 28.
[9] Conference on the priesthood, Maredret, July 8th, 1914.

splendours so that they might be reproduced in some measure in his own life in imitation of the Word Incarnate.

"Ecce Venio"

The Abbot of Maredsous used often return to one of his favourite texts from the Epistle to the Hebrews, which expresses admirably the fundamental attitude of Christ the Priest, coming into the world;

> "Sacrifice and oblation thou wouldst not; but a body thou hast fitted to me
> Holocausts for sin did not please thee
> Then, said I, behold I come (Ecce venio): in the head of the book it is written of me; that I should do thy will, O God. In the which will we are sanctified by the oblation of the body of Jesus Christ once."[10]

These notable verses, which affirm the rejection of the sacrifices of the Old Law, the priestly vocation of the Messias, and the reply of the Son Incarnate to the command of the Father, have had a profound effect on Christian tradition and find an answering echo to-day in the heart of the priest. The mystical genius of St. Michael Garicoits made it the dominating idea of his priestly spirituality, and he sought to make of every member of his institute a living, permanent *Ecce Venio*, completely identified with the inner movements of the Heart of Jesus.

Dom Marmion reacted to this text, not as the founder of an order, but as a contemplative theologian. He saw in this initial gesture of the Word Incarnate the orientation of His whole existence as Christ and of His death to redeem mankind. "In this first oblation Jesus embraced the whole series of actions which made up His life. All that He did from this moment until He drew His last breath on earth was simply the accomplishment and natural development of this first act. That is why St. Paul could say that all the worth of the life

[10] Heb. x, 5-10.

and sufferings of Jesus Christ was contained in advance and, so to speak, *in radice,* in this first oblation."[11]
"This inaugural act was the key of His whole life."

The Sacrifice of the Cross

All the actions of the Word Incarnate, all the sentiments of His heart, assumed a sacerdotal character in view of their orientation towards the redemptive sacrifice. Christ was, so to speak, haunted by the thought of the Cross. This appears from time to time in the Gospels. "He shall be delivered to the Gentiles, and shall be mocked and scourged and spat upon."[12] He had ever before His eyes the betrayal of Judas, the flagellation and all the affronts which the soldiers of Pilate would inflict upon Him. Even on Mount Thabor in the splendour of His glory He spoke of His passion.[13]

In this way Dom Marmion viewed the whole of Christ's life as sacerdotal, but he did not regard the existence of the Word Incarnate as a continuous state of victim beginning with the Incarnation and persevering through the unfolding of the mysteries of this life on earth, to find its consummation in the sacrifice of Heaven. Following the traditional concept, he merely wished to bring out clearly the fact that the redemptive immolation was the culmination of the priesthood of Christ. His whole existence was simply a preparation or an echo of this sacrifice.

As a disciple of St. Paul, Dom Marmion had a keen appreciation of the Cross and of its dominant position in the economy of salvation. His writings are full of flashes of illumination on the mystery of Golgotha. "Cavalry is the luminous centre on which God's gaze was fixed even before the Incarnation; it is the sole source from which the divine mercies flow down on the world."

Thus, by way of merit and of adoration, by way of thanksgiving, expiation and supplication, but always in the form of sacrifice, that is to say, in a form which is essentially sacerdotal,

[11] Conference to priests, Dinant, June 1897.
[12] Luke xviii, 32.   [13] Luke ix, 31.

the sacrifice of Calvary is the supreme act of the priesthood of Christ.

The Sacrifice of the Altar

Christ left to the Church a memorial of His redemptive sacrifice so that He might remain with her in an act of perpetual oblation to His Father and so apply to every generation the infinite fruits of the redemption of the Cross, and unite them by their personal offering with this, the essential act of Christian worship. This is the explanation of the Sacrifice of the altar.

In full accord with the dogmatic teaching of the Council of Trent, Dom Marmion appreciated keenly the close union between the altar and the cross. " The sacrifice of the Mass and that of Calvary constitute one and the same sacrifice. The same Christ who offered Himself once on the cross with the shedding of blood is contained and immolated here in a bloodless manner. But it is one and the same victim. Only the manner of oblation is different." By the consecration of the host we present before the eyes of the eternal Father the death which Christ endured once for the whole human race. For God there is no past or future. He lives in the eternal present. When the sacred species are consecrated, the whole drama of Calvary is unfolded before the eyes of God.

In this unceasing offering of His Sacrifice, Christ remains the Priest of His Church on earth, offering Himself to His Father for the salvation of the world and enabling men to participate, according to the degree of their fervour, in all the benefits of His redemption.

The Eternal Priesthood

In Heaven Christ remains a Victim and a Priest for all eternity. Not that there is, in the strict sense, a sacrifice in Heaven. The one sacrifice of the Cross is perpetuated only by the Eucharist and will cease with the sacramental order at the end of time. The blessed are in enjoyment of the unveiled worship of God, in the immediate presence of the Trinity, freed from all the obscurities of faith. They participate, in the full light of glory, in the life of adoration of the priestly soul of Christ. There, the sacrifice consists in adoration amidst chants of joy and triumph. Christ offers Himself to the Father as a victim, but not now as a mutilated victim, but as one glorified, and glorified in proportion to His sufferings and humiliations here on earth.

"I have offered Myself as a victim of expiation and suffering," says Christ in His glory. "In My agony I uttered the cry of distress: 'My soul is sorrowful even unto death', *tristis est anima mea usque ad mortem*.[14] On the Cross, I cried: 'My God, My God, why hast Thou abandoned me.'" Now everything is changed, and "according to the multitude of My sorrows in My heart, O My Father, Thy comforts have given joy to My soul."[15] There is an eternal consolation corresponding to each one of the sufferings of Jesus, a new exaltation for each of His humiliations. "Christ humbled Himself . . . for which cause God also hath exalted Him and hath given Him a name which is above all names, that in the name of Jesus every knee should bow and every tongue should confess that the Lord Jesus Christ is in the glory of God the Father."[16]

In the consummation of His glory amidst the blessed redeemed by His Blood, Christ triumphs in the splendour of His eternal priesthood.

We have thus the completion of the dogmatic outlook of Dom Marmion. The priesthood of the Word Incarnate has its prototype in the Trinity, its roots in the hypostatic union and its nature lies in the office of mediation of the Man-God. Finally, we have it consummated in the sacrifice of the Cross which is perpetuated on the altar, and its supreme development in eternal glory.

[14] Matt. xxvi, 38. [15] Ps. xciii, 19. [16] Phil. ii, 8-11.

2. THE PRIESTHOOD IN
THE CHURCH

Dignity and Power of the Priest

In assessing the dignity and power of the priest Dom Marmion considered Christ, in whom the priesthood of the Church finds its origin, its model and its efficacy. Before ascending to Heaven, the Word Incarnate chose men to perpetuate His mission on earth. The sacrament of Ordination is, as it were, a prolongation of the Incarnation. The man who receives it becomes in all truth another Christ. In virtue of the character imprinted on his soul the priest reproduces the very Person of the Son in the eyes of His Father. God can say of him as He said of Jesus: " This is my well beloved Son ", *Hic est Filius meus dilectus.*[1] This is the wondrous effect of ordination."[2]

So close is this identification of the priest with Christ that he speaks and acts always in the person of Christ, *in persona Christi.*

On the day of ordination, as at the hour of the Incarnation of the Word, the Blessed Trinity impresses on the soul of the newly ordained priest the ineffaceable seal which marks him as the minister of Christ. " At the moment that the Blessed Virgin pronounced her Fiat, the Holy Ghost came upon her, the Word was made flesh, and the eternal Father, contemplating His Son with an infinite complacency, acknowledged Him as His only-begotten Son and His Priest in these words: ' Thou art My Son, this day have I begotten Thee. Thou art a priest for ever.'[3]

" In like manner, at the moment when the pontiff of the Church laid his hands on our heads, the Holy Ghost came upon us, and the Father looked on us with love and complacency, and saw in us the image of His Son, for the priest is another Christ. At this moment a sublime, superabundant

---

[1] Matt. iii, 17; xvii, 5. Luke ix, 35; II Peter i, 17.
[2] Retreat, Maredret, December 1921.   [3] Heb. v, 5-6.

grace flowed into our souls, consecrating our whole being to the glory of God.

"This grace of ordination consecrates irrevocably to God all that there is in the priest: his body, his soul, his heart and all his affections, and raises them to a plane which is almost infinitely above this world. By virtue of this grace the priest is raised above the angels: *Cui enim dixit aliquando angelorum: Filius es tu . . . et ad angelos quidem dixit: qui facit angelos suos spiritus et ministros.*[4] The angels are simply the ministers of the Lord, while Jesus is His Son. We can say of the priest what St. Paul said of Christ in the Epistle to the Hebrews. He calls the angels His servants but He calls you, priests, His Sons."

"All the sublime dignity of the priest is derived from this identification with Christ. In the eyes of the world he is an ordinary man; in the eyes of the unbeliever he is a contemptible being hardly worthy of the consideration or the rights accorded to the least of men. And yet what sublime privileges are attached to this fragile vessel. *Assimilatus Filio Dei*[5] : by his ordination he has been made like to the Son of God. This other Christ conceals under the appearance of an ordinary man the ineffable gift of his priesthood. In the holy Sacrifice of the Mass the priest is raised to a dignity which is, in a certain sense, divine, because Jesus Christ identifies Himself with His priest in an ineffable manner. At the moment of the consecration Christ and His priest are one. Oh the unspeakable dignity of the priest!

"The supreme dignity of the priest lies in his power to offer Christ in sacrifice to the holy Trinity in the name of the whole Church. *Suscipe Sancta Trinitas.*"

Dom Marmion, as a contemplative soul, had a very keen appreciation of this vital power of our priesthood. He felt, and rightly, that the primary function of the priest was the Mass, in which he perpetuates among men the redemptive sacrifice which has saved the world, and associates the Church militant with the infinite praise of the Word Incarnate. "If a priest did nothing but offer this holy sacrifice every morning, even though he only offered it once in his life—he would

---

[4] Heb. i, 5-6.   [5] Heb. vii, 3.

have done something infinitely greater than all those great actions which excite the admiration of men, for this infinite glory given to God will be eternal like God Himself, while the greatest works of men must pass away. Nothing is eternal except the divine."

Ordination confers on priests another power over the mystical body of Christ. It is his mission to communicate to men the benefits of the redemption. "For as he ascends the steps of the altar he bears the whole Church in his heart, and from the chalice which he consecrates he pours out infinite graces and blessings on all the members of that Church." But the rôle of the priest is not confined exclusively to the celebration of the divine worship; Christ has entrusted His whole Church to the apostles and their successors with the mission of evangelizing it, of sanctifying it and of leading it into the mansion of the Father: 'Going, therefore, teach ye all nations, baptizing them in the name of the Father and of the Son and of the Holy Ghost, teaching them to observe all things whatsoever I have commanded you.'[6]

Dom Marmion was familiar with the great variety of works which a priest must face in the service of men: he had so often undertaken them. The priest is the collaborator of Christ in all the work of the redemption and, like Him, he is priest, doctor, and shepherd of souls. The priest's ideal must not be limited by human standards; it must aspire to the divine. The Founder of the Church has placed in his hands the keys of the kingdom. In this weak man there is a power which is divine. He speaks and the heavens obey. At his word the Son of God comes down on the altar to be immolated at his hands for the glory of His Father and for the salvation of the world. The sinner, weighed down under the burden of a life of sin, kneels before him, and the priest, speaking once more in the name of this God who dwells within him, says: "I forgive you your sins. Go in peace." The criminal, worthy a moment ago to be cast into hell, rises pardoned and justified, for the word of the priest is a word of divine power. From the time of His glorious ascension Christ's place on earth is filled by the priest; and it is by his ministry that Christ

---

[6] Matt. xxviii, 19-20.

sanctifies every stage of our mortal life from our baptism until we receive those final consolations with which the Church surrounds the last moments of her children.

How clearly Dom Marmion could elaborate this idea of his rôle as priest, doctor and shepherd! He is "the light of the world";[7] it is from his lips that men receive the teaching of revelation and the precepts of the divine law. The Abbot of Maredsous attached the utmost importance to this mission of priests to evangelize the world. It is for the priest also to lead the flock of Christ to the highest perfection. He is the director of souls. "In unhappy Ireland, my native country, which has endured three centuries of persecution unparalleled in the annals of history, not only has the priest preserved the faith inviolate but he has always been the comforter and the best friend of the people."[8]

Finally, having offered Christ to His Father, the priest gives this same Christ to souls. These are the two aspects of his priestly office. "The great function of the priest," says Dom Marmion in conclusion, "is to give Jesus Christ to the world."

Priestly holiness

With Dom Marmion the most elevated dogmatic consideration always culminate in a directive for life and for action. The multiple perspectives of his spiritual doctrine are so closely united in the person of Christ that it is easy to deduce from it his teaching on priestly sanctity. For him, the priest is the Christian most closely resembling Christ.

Fundamental principle
Sacerdos alter Christus

The traditional formula, *Sacerdos alter Christus* expresses admirably the thought of Dom Marmion, whose Christocentrism is the motif of his whole teaching. It is the dominating idea in his priestly spirituality. By Baptism and Confirmation the Christian bears the mark of Christ, but the sacrament

[7] Matt. v, 14.   [8] Sermon for a First Mass, between 1902-1909.

of Holy Orders imprints on his whole being "the greatest possible resemblance to Christ, accomplishing in him the final evolution of the sacrament of Baptism."

"On the day of his ordination, after having received the sacerdotal anointing, he rises transformed into another Christ." He has been endowed with His power and he must assume His sanctity and His interior sentiments. As the priest is another Christ by virtue of the powers bestowed on him, he must be another Christ also in the dispositions of his soul. His whole sanctity consists in identifying himself with Christ. As he goes on in life he must disappear more and more to give place to Christ. Gradually this divine fire will destroy in him all that is sin, all that is imperfect, and he will live only in Christ. Like St. Paul, he will then be able to say: "I live now, not I, but Christ liveth in me."

Eminent Sanctity of the Priest

Like his illustrious friend Cardinal Mercier, Dom Marmion made it his particular aim to awaken in priests a full appreciation of the transcendency of their priesthood. He wanted to see in them dispositions similar to those of Christ. "There is no more fatal error," he used to say, "than to lower the priestly ideal. If the priest thinks that he can be satisfied with the measure of sanctity of ordinary Christians, that it is enough for him to avoid mortal sin, that he is not bound to aim any higher than this, he runs a great danger of losing his soul. Even if he succeeds in saving his soul, he will have passed his whole life without experiencing those intimate joys which God reserves to His priests, and without having accomplished the great work which God expected of him when He bestowed upon him the grace of the priesthood." The state of grace of his priesthood gives him a soul like to that of Christ, the Mediator, the worshipper of the Father, and the redeemer of souls. This grace of Ordination, like the hypostatic union, is the source of all the gifts, of all the powers which raise the priest almost infinitely above the ordinary Christian. It identifies him with Christ in the intimacy of

His relations with the Father. Herein lies hidden the most profound secret of the interior life of the priest, as is the case also for the Son of God. "He participates in the greatest measure in all that is most holy and most sublime in Jesus Christ: His priestly ministry before the Father. After the model of Christ the priest must always be the perfect adorer and glorifier of the Father."

Dom Marmion's concept of the priest, of the sublimity of his powers, and the eminence of his sanctity is very elevated. He sees him invested by delegation with the power and the sanctity of Christ. Dom Marmion had meditated a great deal on the texts of the Pontifical in which the Church, in the ceremonies of ordination, outlines for the priest the ideal of perfection to which he must aspire. "Let all sanctity shine forth in him," *Eluceat in eis totius forma justitiae.* The priest must be clothed in all the virtues: the perfection of charity towards God and his neighbour, heavenly wisdom, justice, constancy, mercy, fortitude, a high degree of probity, wisdom, a mature gravity in his conduct and his works, perfect faith, exemplary chastity. Finally, in all circumstances he must exhibit that integrity of a holy life which makes the Church, the spouse of Christ, rejoice in the virtues of her priest."

The Abbot of Maredsous was keenly aware of the transcendent perfection which the good of the Church requires in her priests. In virtue of his sublime function at the altar and his rôle as the sanctifier of souls the priest is called by God to a higher sanctity than all the other members of the mystical body. The Abbot of Maredsous reminds us on this point of the teaching of St. Thomas who merely resumes the doctrine of the Fathers of the Church when he says: "Although externally the religious state is more perfect than that of the priest, his interior sanctity should surpass that of the religious.[9] If he has the charge of souls his sanctity should far exceed that of a simple priest religious. This grace of ordination is so abundant that, provided it encounters no obstacle, it can raise

---

[9] Quia per sacrum ordinem aliquis deputatur ad dignissima mysteria, quibus ipsi Christo servitur in sacramento altaris; ad quod requiritur major sanctitas interior, quam requirat etiam religionis status, 11 11 184, 8.

the simplest souls to the highest degree of sanctity: as for
example, the curé d'Ars."[10]

In accordance with the traditional doctrine of the Church,
Dom Marmion never failed to insist on the transcendence of
priestly sanctity over all other forms of Christian perfection.

Spirit of Faith

In Dom Marmion's teaching on the priesthood we find the
fundamental theses of his spiritual doctrine adapted to the life
of the priest. How could it be otherwise with a man whose
doctrine was an integral part of his life?

As the basis of everything, he requires an ardent faith in
Jesus Christ. "Nothing can take the place of this faith in
Jesus Christ, for it is the very essence of our priesthood to be
worthy members of Jesus Christ: '*Sic nos existimet homo ut
ministros Christi et dispensatores mysteriorum Dei.*'"[11]

Faith is the great fundamental virtue of the priest. It is
the root which must maintain, support, and nourish continuously the life of his soul.

All our priestly activities must be exercised in an atmosphere of faith and they will increase in value according as we
advance in the spiritual life. Without faith the existence of
the priest would be a mere pretence. "God has put in our
hands the most potent means to do great things for His glory.
There is no limit to the results which these means may produce in the salvation of souls, but by a law of providence these
results depend in great measure on the dispositions of those
who employ them. All the value of our life, therefore, depends
on our faith. God will require us to render a strict account
of the infinite riches which He has entrusted to us. It is
through us that Jesus Christ must be given to the world, but
for that it is necessary that He dwell in our hearts by faith:
Christum habitare per fidem in cordibus nostris."[12]

If they have not got this ardent faith the priests will, indeed,
administer the sacraments validly in virtue of their ordination,
but they will not attain to Christ themselves. The priest must

---

[10] Conference to priests, Denant, before March 1899.
[11] I Cor. iv, 1.   [12] Eph. iii, 17.

be the first to believe in the priesthood and in this identification with Christ as the instruments of the communication of
His grace.

The rôle of faith is of primary importance in the life of
the priest to enable him to escape from the aridity of routine
or naturalism, and to maintain the supernatural note in his
ministry. Failing this, his work is merely a form of activism.
"Faith must be the foundation and the principle of our life
if we wish it to be meritorious: *sine fide impossible est placere
Deo.*[13] St. Catherine of Siena says that every step that we
advance in perfection must be accompanied by an increase in
faith. The more our life is a life of faith, the more supernatural it will be, and the more pleasing to God. The
salvation of souls and the sanctification of the world are matters
which are essentially supernatural, and no human activity,
unless it is made fruitful by grace and by the divine anointing,
is capable of converting or sanctifying a single soul. That is
why the saints, who see all things with the eyes of faith, while
employing all their energy in their good works, rely much
more on prayer and the help of grace. This explains why two
of the most active saints of modern times, St. Francis de Sales
and St. Alphonsus Liguori, founded two orders of contemplative nuns and, if I may be permitted to speak of my own
forerunners in the monastic order, those great monks who
converted Europe have always begun by founding a monastery
as a centre of prayer, of grace, and of light from which the
grace of faith radiated forth on the surrounding population."

This spirit of faith enables the priest to see God everywhere
as the blessed contemplate God and see all things in the light
of His divinity. They see the signs of God in everything. In
like manner the man of faith perceives a thousand things of
which the unbeliever has no suspicion: the world of redemption and sanctifying grace, the status of members of the body
of Christ and temples of the Holy Ghost, the infinite riches
of Jesus Christ, etc."

"The faith of the priest is not a cold philosophic faith, but
a living faith which casts us in adoration at the feet of Christ:
It makes an immolation of our intelligence to the Word.

[13] Heb. xi, 6.

It delivers us up unreservedly to His Will.

It gives us unbounded confidence in His merits.

It makes us see Jesus Christ in our neigbour, His authority in our superiors, His grandeur in the saints, His needs in the members of His mystical body."

Dom Marmion sought with jealous care to maintain this living faith in the heart of priests. He warned them of the great danger of evil reading or even of worldly reading. Those who were habitually occupied in studying the classics were especially in need of a corrective: they needed to live by faith.

In his pastoral retreats he insisted particularly on one point: the faith of the priest must be an enlightened faith for, as he explained, the movement of the heart follows the knowledge of the intellect: *ignoti nulla cupido*. If we know God and His perfections, if we are penetrated with the appreciation of His majesty, His grandeur, His goodness and His mercy; if by faith we have made the submission of our intelligence to all these great truths, God will proceed from our intelligence into our heart. This point is of capital importance. The heart of the priest must be a furnace of immense love for God, a love which is not a mere sensible impression, but a spirit of faith enlightened by study and a theological knowledge of God.

It follows from this that study must play a big part in the life of the priest. "We must apply ourselves with great zeal to the study of the sacred sciences, not with the object of being known as great scholars; '*ut sciantur ipsi est turpis vanitas*', as St. Bernard says. For those who work in this spirit their study becomes a source, not of sanctity, but of pride and danger. It is of knowledge acquired with this object that the Holy Spirit has said, '*scientia inflat*',[14] and of which it is written again: '*Sapientia huius saeculi stultitia est apud Deum*.'[15] We might add 'apud homines' for there is nothing more contemptible and pitiable than a priest who is filled with the idea of his own learning. We must never let ourselves be dazzled by our knowledge. We must apply ourselves to study for the glory of God so that we may be in a position

[14] I Cor. viii, 1.   [15] I Cor. iii, 19.

to defend the Church and to preserve the faith in all its purity and strength in the hearts of the faithful. Above all, our object must be to fill our own hearts with the knowledge of Jesus Christ and the sublime mysteries of the faith which produce in us that living theology which is the soul of priestly sanctity." On another occasion he expresses the same thought in the magnificent formula: "The clergy should be a living theology."[16]

By study I do not mean the reading of little manuals, useful as these may be as a preparation for the examination for ordination, but rather the study of the great masters of the sacred sciences: St. Thomas, St. Bonaventure, the Fathers of the Church, and above all else, the Scriptures. The Scriptures are the great treasure of the Church. It was by the study and meditation of the sacred books that the Fathers of the Church and the greatest theologians were formed. They will be until the end of time the primary source of the sacred sciences. The priest who studies and loves the Holy Scriptures will always have in his soul and in his heart a living fountain of inspiration guiding him to eternal life.

In this, as in everything, we must begin with the dry, painful side of study, resigning ourselves in the beginning to seeing nothing and feeling nothing but the labour of study. We shall be amply recompensed in due time. Without this labour our whole life will be passed in the outer darkness. How many priests are there who speak of the sacred mysteries without understanding them, without thinking about them, without even knowing them. They pass their life surrounded by holy things, and in constant contact with the supernatural powers, at the altar, in the confessional, in the pulpit, without giving their mind to them, and without deriving the least profit for their own souls. The priest dispenses so many graces which must of necessity pass through his own heart before they reach the faithful by his hands. If he has not got that enlightened faith, that theological piety, these graces will not affect him, will not bring warmth to his own heart; he will remain famished in the midst of abundance. We must follow the example of St. Thomas and never study without praying.

[16] Retreat to priests, Louvain, 1898.

" This spirit of faith is the root and foundation of our whole spiritual life, the source of the fruitfulness of our priestly life. The priest requires a much stronger faith than that of the ordinary faithful.

" The faith of a people degenerates quickly into superstition if it is not enlightened and maintained by the learning and the instruction of the clergy . . . I feel bound to stress this point particularly in addressing you, for this great University of Louvain has stood for centuries as a centre of learning and orthodoxy."[17]

And, in support of these practical counsels, the theologian rises, as was his habit, to the most sublime considerations, letting his contemplative thought be carried away in the splendid light of the Word. " If the heart of Jesus is the centre of the infinite love of the Word," he concludes, " it is also the heart of Him who is ' eternal Wisdom proceeding from the Most High,' *Sapientia quae ex ore altissimi prodiit.*"[18]

The Virtue of Religion

It was not surprising that the Benedictine spirit of Dom Marmion should lay great stress on the special part which the virtue of religion must play in the whole life of the priest. The priest is, above all else, a man of God, a minister of Christian worship. " As priests, we must be steeped in this spirit of religion, which is simply a feeling of great humility and self-abasement in face of the infinite majesty of God. Just as the sacred humanity of Jesus, in virtue of the hypostatic union, was consecrated and immolated in its entirety to the glory of His Father so that in Him every action, even the most indifferent in themselves, constituted sublime acts of the virtue of religion, so also, our whole being, by virtue of our ordination, has been consecrated to the glory of God. In us, everything, even the most indifferent actions must be acts of the virtue of religion, priestly acts."[19] This spirit of religion is " the characteristic virtue of the priest ".[20]

[17] Priests' retreat, Louvain, 1898.   [18] Eccles. xxiv, 3.
[19] Conferences to priests, Dinant, 1897.
[20] Retreat to priests, Louvain, October 1898.

His conferences to priests are a veritable treasure house on this subject. One feels that they are penetrated by all the conviction which is the fruit of a Benedictine life. "The priest does not cease to be a priest when he leaves the altar. He must remain a priest everywhere and in all circumstances. He has been chosen primarily for divine worship: 'Every high priest taken from among men, is ordained for men in the things that appertain to God.'[21] This is his *raison d'être,* his primary duty. Like the Master he can say: 'Did you not know that I must be about My Father's business.'"[22] And to the forgetful and the negligent the Abbot of Maredsous would offer the brief, pointed advice: "Before anything else, be priests."[23] This was his ideal: everywhere and always, a priest.

The Priest's Mass

The Mass plays an outstanding part in the life of a priest. The offering of the Eucharistic sacrifice is for the priest the occasion of his supreme identification with Christ; it is the time when he has most power for the good of souls, when he is most useful to the whole mystical body. "His dispositions must be the same as those of Jesus, Priest and Victim."[24] "In union with Christ, the Supreme Pontiff, he fulfils perfectly all his duties towards the Father: adoration, thanksgiving, expiation and impetration. The priest, being identified with Christ, attains the highest degree of adoption possible here on earth." [25] The offering of the sacrifice of the Mass is for the priest "the great means of transformation into Christ".[26]

"All the sacerdotal activity of the priest must be carried out in the spirit of the Mass. We can measure the fervour of a priest by his Mass. Consider two priests going up to the altar. Let us suppose that they are both in the state of grace. One leaves the altar filled with the love of God and as St. John Chrysostom says: *spirans flammas, daemonibus terribilis.* His heart is filled with joy; God is with him and it is his

[21] Heb. v, 1.   [22] Luke ii, 49.
[23] Conferences to priests, Louvain, 1902-3.
[24] Retreat, Maredret, December 1921.
[25] Retreat to priests, Louvain, November 1901.   [26] Ibidem.

N

happiness to be with God. The other leaves the altar cold of heart, distracted, discouraged, without strength or energy. The quarter hour of thanksgiving seems to him to last for ever. He can find nothing in his heart to say to Our Lord. What is the reason for this difference? The Mass was the same. The first priest was full of the virtue of religion, while the second was entirely devoid of it."

As a master of the spiritual life Dom Marmion did not allow himself to be dazzled by talent or the glitter of genius. The priest of Jesus Christ is able to give God to his fellow men according to the measure of his own sanctity. The secret of all apostolic work lies in union with God. This divine intimacy is the basis of the priestly spirit.

The Spirit of Prayer

If the priest wishes to be faithful to the grace of his priesthood, to his two-fold mission as glorifier of the Father and sanctifier of souls, he must be a man of prayer. Without the spirit of prayer no deep supernatural life is possible. Priestly duties need to be carried out in a spirit of prayer. Of all the means, prayer is the most necessary; it must be the foundation and, as it were, the very breath of our soul. It is by this constant recourse of the priest to God that he can be assured of His continuous help. "The man who is united to God by a life of prayer becomes a focus of grace, of light, and of peace for all who approach him. Why is this? Because all his natural powers are, so to speak, divinized, raised to a plane which is almost infinitely above nature. Through grace the Holy Ghost becomes the inspirer of his thoughts, of his words, of his actions. All the same, man remains weak, imperfect, and sometimes buffeted by violent temptations so that—as we are told by St. Paul, who was a living example of this truth —he may recognize that the marvels which he does do not come from him, and that no flesh may glorify itself in His presence. *Ut non glorificetur omnis caro in conspectu eius,*[27] *ut sublimitas sit ex Deo et non ex nobis.*[28, 29]

[27] I Cor. i, 29.   [28] II Cor. iv, 7.
[29] Conferences to priests, Dinant, August 1897.

" There is no excuse for us. If we remain weak, if we make no progress, if we fall into sin, if we lose our souls, the reason is that we have not troubled to seek the necessary strength and graces in the inexhaustible divine treasures which are always accessible to us by prayer."

The life of prayer, for the priest, finds its daily expression in the recitation of the breviary, provided that he is not content to mumble hastily a few psalms, but unites himself with the whole Church in the praise of the Word. The country parish priest, and the missioner who is praying alone in the bush, speak in the name of the Church: *os totius Ecclesiae*.[30] By virtue of this constant recitation of the Divine Office the whole Church is in a state of continuous prayer before God. " The Church does not confine herself to recommending the priest to be a man of prayer; she prescribes for him the form in which he is to carry out his obligation. Except for assistance at Mass and the reception of the sacraments, the prayer of the ordinary layman is left to his own private devotion; but the prayer of the priest is so important for the good of the Church and for the salvation of souls that she appoints for him that prayer which is most pleasing to God, most efficacious for us, most fruitful in grace and in light: the prayer of the Liturgy which comprises the Divine Office and the Mass.

" A priest who recites his breviary and celebrates his Mass devoutly will be a holy priest and will do much for the glory of God, while the priest who is negligent in regard to these great duties of his state will be lacking in fervour and without any interior life; he will have little influence on souls.

" I am not confounding sanctity with prayer, which is only a means to sanctity, but I know that the priest who is faithful in this matter will receive so much light from God, so much grace and strength, that he cannot fail to make great progress. When St. Joseph de Cupertino was consulted by a bishop as to how he could sanctify his clergy, he replied: see to it that your priests recite their breviary devoutly and say their Mass well, and I will answer for the rest."[31]

[30] Retreat to priests, Tournai, August 1922.
[31] Conferences to priests, Louvain, 1922-23.

The Other Priestly Virtues

All the Christian virtues should shine forth in the priest. Dom Marmion was very conscious of this and insisted on the practice of this or that virtue according to the circumstances and in particular on the practice of the greatest of the theological virtues, charity. The heart of the priest must be filled with an immense love for God and for souls. *Christ the Ideal of the Priest* contains much that is valuable on this point.

There were two priestly virtues to which the Abbot of Maredsous attached especial importance: the spirit of detachment, and obedience. The priesthood requires complete abnegation. The priest is, as it were, a man cut off. "He leaves the family and the joys of the home. It is no longer lawful for him even to desire these things. It would be a sacrilege on his part. He renounces the right to dispose of his own person or his time."[32] He lives in a "virginal solitude on a plane far above all human love".[33] He must pass through the world "detached from all that is of the world".[34]

Freed by this act of renouncement from the burden of his own person and of worldly goods, the priest belongs wholly to God, entirely devoted to the service of the Church and of souls. The virtue of obedience makes him the invaluable collaborator of the bishop. Abbot Marmion, who had a keen supernatural appreciation of the hierarchic order in the Church, urged very strongly the importance of submission to authority in accordance with the counsel of St. Ignatius of Antioch: "Do nothing without the approval of the bishop."[35] "At your ordination you promised obedience to your bishop. I know that this obedience is not as absolute or as radical as religious obedience; it is the obedience of the apostles. You made this promise to your bishop at the most solemn moment of your life in the presence of God and before the altar on which you had just offered for the first time the holy sacrifice together with the bishop who had ordained you. By this promise you gave the bishop the right to dispose of your per-

---

[32] Conferences to priests, Dinant, before 1899.   [33] Ibidem, July 1897.
[34] Retreat to priests, Louvain, 1898.   [35] Eph. iv.

son, to place you where he thinks fit, to move you from one place to another, and to give you whatever work he wishes. This constitutes a sacrifice which is extremely meritorious and agreeable to God. The greatest thing which a man possesses is his liberty and the right to dispose of his person and determine his activity. Nothing can deprive man of this right; it is a right respected by God Himself. Even when He leads man by the most powerful graces, He leaves his liberty inviolate. Now, by this promise that we have made, we have handed over for the love of God our person, our talents and all our activity to the bishop for the good of the Church."[36]

A clergy which is subject to its bishop in the common effort in the service of souls constitutes an invincible team and will achieve wonders in the work of the apostolate. "It may be said of a diocese, as of a religious community, that its strength lies in the obedience of its priests." Each individual priest gains from it, personally, the certainty of doing the will of God and of finding an infallible way to achieve sanctity.

"In this way," Dom Marmion declared, "the life of Jesus becomes our life, and, even in our most indifferent actions, we can say like Christ: 'I do always those things which are pleasing to My Father.'"[37]

Christ, the Ideal of the Priest

Like all the other aspects of his spirituality, the ascetic doctrine of Dom Marmion on the priesthood is dominated by Christ.

The priesthood of the Church originates in the Word Incarnate; in Him it finds its model; from Him it derives its efficacy. The priest, who is another Christ by virtue of the power he exercises in his sacred functions, must enter into the interior dispositions of the Son of God and be another Christ before God and before men. Of all members of the mystical body it is the priest who is called to the most perfect identification with Christ.

This central idea of the spirituality of Dom Marmion achieves its fullest development in his ascetic doctrine on the

---

[36] Conferences to priests, 1904-6.   [37] John viii, 29.

priesthood. "For me Jesus Christ is everything. I cannot celebrate Mass or exercise any priestly function except in complete dependence on Him and on His Holy Spirit."[38]

When the time came to offer the Holy Sacrifice, as he put on the vestments, his soul entered into a close union with that of Christ. Everything else ceased to exist for him. "I feel that through the Church I enter into close union with Jesus, the great High Priest, and with her and through her I share in the dispositions of Jesus Christ."[39]

One day the Abbot of Maredsous went to a church in Belgium and asked if he might celebrate Mass. The sacristan was hurrying to lay out the vestments for him, when the parish priest happened to come into the sacristy and wanted to know the name of the celebrant. Getting impatient, he began to press the sacristan, saying "Who is it that is going to say Mass." Dom Marmion intervened quietly: "Jesus Christ."

[38] Letter to Mother Garnier, December 2nd, 1908.
[39] Letter to a Carmelite nun, April 4th, 1917.

V

THE MOTHER OF CHRIST

Marian Christo-centrism – The divine Maternity – The
Immaculate Conception – Fulness of grace – Mediatrix of all
graces – Behold your Mother! – Personal intimacy with Mary

To be for Mary another Jesus

V

THE MOTHER OF CHRIST

THERE is a law of religious psychology which may be observed in all the saints, that their relation with Mary follows the form of their spiritual life. For Dom Marmion this relation is a radiation of the mystery of Christ.

Marian Christo-centrism

For him Mary is above all else the Mother of Jesus whose mission it is to form us in His image. She is the Mother of the only begotten Son and Mother also of the multitude of the children of adoption. In a word she is the Mother of the whole Christ.

While many souls go to Jesus through Mary, Dom Marmion approaches the Mother through Christ. No better formula can be found to characterize this approach so typical of his spirituality than " Marian Christo-centrism ". For him everything, even in the mystery of Mary, is dominated by Christ.

In his private notes, the young monk of Maredsous gives some indications—too rare indeed, but all the more precious for that—of his inner devotion to Mary. We find him emphasizing its connection with the basic principle of his whole spiritual life. " On the feast of Our Lady of the Seven Dolours and on the feast of the Blessed Virgin Mary de Mercede, I felt a great increase of devotion towards the Blessed Virgin. Our perfection is in just proportion to our resemblance to Jesus Christ. ' This is My beloved Son in whom I well pleased.' The love and reverence of Jesus for His blessed Mother were immense. Therefore I must try to imitate Him in this. This is especially true of a priest who is 'alter Christus'."[1]

The whole spiritual process of Dom Columba is clearly set out for us in this passage. He has but one ideal: to imitate Christ. He approaches the Mother therefore with the sentiments of an 'alter Christus'. Later, to express the fundamental law of this inner devotion to Mary he conceives a formula as expressive as it is concise: "We must be by grace what Jesus is by nature, a child of God and a child of Mary. God will recognize as His true children only those who, like Jesus, are children of Mary."[2] Christ, the exemplary cause of our predestination, must be the model of our divine sonship and of our sonship to Mary. The whole doctrine of Dom Marmion is thus centred in a synthesis which attaches his concept of Mary to that central thought in which his spirituality finds its unity and its strength: the all-important place of Christ in God's plan.

The Divine Maternity

As in all his work, the mystery of Mary is illuminated from above by the dogmatic approach of Dom Marmion. He sees her, above all else, as the Mother of God. As a theologian he sees here the secret of all the graces and all the privileges of Mary. This is for him the supreme principle of Mariology.

When teaching his students he used to insist on this fundamental principle: "We have here the basis of all this doctrine: the divine Maternity of Mary, although subsequent in its realization in time, is the ultimate reason, the eminent source of all the graces and prerogatives of Mary. Everything flows from it."

He admired the Marian doctrine of St. Thomas because of the predominance in it of the divine Maternity. He had meditated at length on the classic texts, to which he used gladly return: "There are three things which are on the fringe of the infinite: the hypostatic union, the divine Maternity, our beatitude. God cannot achieve anything

---

[1] *Private Notes*, September 1888.
[2] Sermon at the Carmel, Louvain, July 16th, 1899.

greater."[3] "According to St. Thomas," he used to repeat,
"it would be impossible for God Himself to create a higher
dignity. This is the highest dignity which He could have conferred on Mary. It raises her above all other creatures. 'All
creatures shall call me blessed, because the Almighty hath
done great things to me,' *Beatam me dicent omnes genera-
tiones quia fecit mihi magna qui potens est*."[4]

Everything in Mary therefore is related to her divine Maternity, the keystone of all her greatness. On the feasts of the
Immaculate Conception and the other liturgical feasts, Dom
Marmion traces back all the glories of Mary to this fundamental dogma. "Mary is the Mother of God. This is the
greatest of her glories, the first of her prerogatives. That is
why she is immaculate. It was fitting that this blessed creature,
destined to bear in her chaste womb the Son of God Himself,
should not for a single instant be under the dominion of the
demon. Mary, the Mother of God, could not be other than
immaculate. The one follows naturally from the other."[5]

The primacy of the divine Maternity, illuminating the
whole mystery of the Mother of Christ, was the culmination of
his Mariology: "Those who question the grandeur of Mary
have never appreciated the full significance of those words of
the Gospel: 'Mary of whom was born Jesus.'"[6]

The Immaculate Conception

The first and most splendid of these divine gifts which
derived from this divine maternity was the Immaculate
Conception.

In 1904, the fiftieth anniversary of the proclamation of this
dogma was the occasion of commemorative celebrations
throughout the Catholic world. Dom Marmion was invited
to give a discourse at Brussels on this glorious privilege of
Mary. He spoke, as always, as a theologian who was accustomed to contemplate the mysteries of the Christian faith in
their highest aspects.

[3] *Summa Theologica* I, xxv, 6, ad 3.
[4] Conference to priests, Dinant, 1897-98.
[5] Conferences to the Carmel of Louvain, December 5th, 1904.
[6] Sermon, Brussels, December 8th, 1904.

Dom Marmion was familiar with the celebrated passage of the bull *Ineffabilis* so remarkable for the conciseness of its doctrine, in which the Church reveals to us the eternal choice predestining Mary, in virtue of the divine predilection, to the supreme dignity of Mother of the Son of God. As she was more loved by God so also was she more richly endowed with the abundance of all graces than the rest of creatures, being indissolubly united to Christ in the one decree of the Incarnation for the redemption of mankind, and clothed in such a plenitude of innocence and sanctity that no mind other than that of God Himself can form an adequate concept of it.

In accordance with this teaching of the Church Dom Marmion liked to consider this mystery of the Immaculate Mary in its eternal origin, in the Holy Trinity, "All the excellences of nature and of grace which we honour in the saints: their perfection, their miracles, their personal grace, their extraordinary gifts, all these are derived from a single source: the adorable Trinity. St. James declares it: 'Every best gift and every perfect gift is from above, coming down from the Father of light.'[7] How could the eminent grandeur and the privileges of Mary be an exception to this rule? No. Everything in her is derived from this essential source of all grace and sanctity."

But Christ is always the one mediator. In accordance with the mind of the Church and with a full appreciation of the sensibility of our Protestant brethren on this fundamental point, Dom Marmion was careful to attribute this exceptional privilege of the Immaculate Conception to the merits of Jesus Christ, the sole Redeemer of the world.

"The Church teaches us that the Immaculate Conception was conferred on Mary *ex morte Filii sui praevisa*: in prevision of the death of her son, just as salvation in the Old Testament was also obtained in virtue of the future sufferings of Christ. What a magnificent gift from the Son of God to His Mother! It was the first fruit of His Passion and consequently a proof of that love than which no one hath greater. It was a privilege surpassing all created power and consequently worthy of the Son of God.

[7] Jas. i, 17.

" With what rapture did Jesus lay at His Mother's feet this royal diadem which He had purchased with His precious blood! With what love, with what gratitude did Mary respond to His loving liberality and consecrate every fibre of her heart to His love!

" But this glorious privilege of Mary was only in view of the glory of Christ, for it is the dawn of that perfect sanctity of Him who was called the Sun of Justice. Before appearing above the horizon, the sun announces its arrival by the glory with which it gilds the mountains; in like manner the Most High, before leaving the bosom of His Father, prepares the tabernacle which was to receive Him for nine months by communicating to it that most stainless purity which was never sullied by the slightest blemish of sin. As we contemplate the Son of God in the bosom of His Father, holy, innocent, purity itself, can we imagine Him born of a Mother sullied by the slightest strain, *Sanctificavit tabernaculum suum altissimus.*[8] He, of whom we say at Holy Mass: *tu solus sanctus, Jesu Christe*, could He be born and receive this human nature but from one who was all pure and immaculate? "[9]

Like a true theologian he goes on to analyse clearly and precisely the nature of this privilege, firstly in its negative aspect: exemption from original sin; then in its positive aspect: the incomparable fulness of grace which raises the immaculate Mary above all the angels and all the saints.

To do this he must enter, by way of introduction, into an exposition of the state of innocence and the first fall. " To understand this doctrine of the Immaculate Conception we must go back to the origins of our race and consider our first parents as they came forth, clothed in justice and innocence, from the hands of their Creator.

" By their disobedience sin entered into their souls and with sin death. But He who commanded the sea and the wind stems this torrent by His almighty Word and forbade the waters of iniquity to touch the soul of her who was to be His Mother. Never, even for an instant, was Mary a child of wrath. The sin of Adam reached her not. She was pure and immaculate. *Tota pulchra es, o Maria.*"

[8] Ps. xlv, 4.   [9] Sermon, Brussels, December 8th, 1904.

While we marvel at this preservation of Mary from all stain of sin, it is the positive aspect of her incomparable fulness of grace which is most important for us. "In order to understand the greatness of this gift which Jesus bestowed on His mother, we must not forget that by the Immaculate Conception is meant, not merely exemption from the stain of sin, but also, and above all, sanctifying grace, a 'partaking of the divine nature'.

"We are destined to be admitted into the bosom of the adorable Trinity, to see God as He sees Himself. Sanctifying grace renders us capable of this sublime elevation, clothing us, as it were, with a robe of justice and beauty, rendering our souls like unto God Himself. This is why, as we chant on the introit of the feast, Mary rejoices with great joy for God hath clothed her with the garment of salvation: *Gaudens gaudebo in Domino.*

"This robe of justice is that sanctifying grace which adorns her soul from the moment of her conception. But in her canticle of praise and gratitude she continues: 'And with a robe of justice He hath covered me like a bride adorned with her jewels.' What are these jewels? The psalmist, enlightened by the Holy Ghost, sings the glories of the future Redeemer: 'Thou art beautiful above the sons of men, grace is poured forth on Thy lips. Therefore hath God blessed Thee for ever. The sceptre of Thy kingdom is a sceptre of righteousness. The queen stood on Thy right hand in gilded clothing surrounded with variety.'[10] The king is Jesus; the queen is Mary."

And the learned preacher displays to us the richness of her immeasurable fulness of grace; an enlightened faith which made her see the eternal Word, the only begotten Son of the Father, under all the mysteries of His humanity; a hope which did not falter even at Golgotha; an immense, boundless love which took possession of her soul and gave to the least of her acts an absolute perfection, an immeasurable value. "All these graces, all those gifts of the Holy Spirit, are attached to her Immaculate Conception. All three Persons of the Blessed Trinity have delighted to shower their gifts on Mary."

[10] Ps. xliv.

And Dom Marmion concluded in a transport of thanksgiving: " Let us therefore unite with Mary: ' My soul doth magnify the Lord.' Glory be to the Father and to the Son and to the Holy Ghost."[11]

Fulness of Grace

We must not expect a complete systematic explanation of Mariology in the doctrine of Dom Marmion. Like the Fathers of the Church he touches on this or that aspect of the Christian mysteries according to the requirements of his immediate purpose and the message he is seeking to convey. Had it not been for the celebrations of the fiftieth anniversary of the proclamation of the dogma of the Immaculate Conception, we should not have these splendid passages which preserve for us the living echo of his personal reaction to this great privilege of Mary.

It is by brief flashes, which escape from him, as it were, according to the circumstances and in the course of his teaching, that we learn how profoundly he had penetrated the mystery of Mary. He sees in her a being who is altogether exceptional, ' more dearly loved by God ',[12] than all the angels and saints and who manifests a sublime simplicity both in her hidden life and in all the great events of her existence. His concept of Mary contains no false marvels. He sees the Mother of God going through life like a woman of our own times, busy about the most ordinary daily tasks; leading a life without ecstasies,[13] and without miracles, but raised to sublime heights of contemplation[14] and in constant union with God.

"The Blessed Virgin was occupied in the most ordinary actions, doing her housekeeping, mending the clothes of St. Joseph, but what love she put into every one of those tasks! "[15] "What a difference between the Blessed Virgin's observance of the Law and the observance of a Pharisee! "[16]

In each of the mysteries of her life he sees a perfect model

---

[11] Sermon, Brussels, December 8th, 1904. [14] Ibidem.
[12] Conference, Maredret, June 23rd, 1910. [15] Retreat, Maredret, 1898.
[13] Retreat, Maredret, February 1914. [16] Retreat, Erdington, 1902.

of sanctity and is lost in wonder at her faith, her humility and her life of love. The *fiat* of the Virgin of Nazareth appears to him as the living synthesis of all her virtues and the "key to her life",[17] providing for Christian souls a splendid example of sanctity. "Your life must be like hers:" *Ecce ancilla Domini*.[18] He used frequently comment with all the vigour of his faith on the well-known prayer of M. Olier: *O Jesu vivens in Maria*. One of the mysteries of the childhood of Jesus which had a special attraction for him was the Presentation. But Dom Marmion did not delay on the mere externals of this mystery, giving it its true setting in the glorious perspective of the redemption of the world. The Virgin, coming to offer her Son to the Father, anticipated, by this gesture of oblation, as in the offertory, the sacrifice which was to be consummated with the shedding of His blood on Golgotha.

And so, on the occasion of the different liturgical feasts, the Abbot of Maredsous in his contemplative soul sees the Mother ever at the side of her Son. They were inseparable in his heart even as they are in the economy of our salvation.

Mediatrix of all graces

Here again—though it was a point very near to his heart—we can only glean fragments of his thought. There remain only a few indications—but happily they are quite explicit—on this question of universal mediation which is so prominent in all studies of Mariology to-day.

As early as 1893 Dom Columba writes in his private notes on the occasion of a retreat: "The conference on the mediation of Mary was excellent. It has filled my heart with confidence and has given me a great desire to become a true child of Mary."[19] When he became in due course a professor and a preacher, he eagerly joined the large number of theologians who taught that all the graces given by God to men pass through the hands of Mary.[20] "God willed to give us His Son

---

[17] Retreat, Maredret, 1901.　　[19] *Private Notes*, September 1893.
[18] Letter, August 1908.　　[20] Retreat to priests, Louvain, October 1898.

through her. In like manner it is His will that every grace and every blessing should come to us through Mary."[21]

While fully appreciating the primary importance of the *fiat* of the Blessed Virgin for the Incarnation, which included her acceptance of her double motherhood, of her rôle as mother of the whole Christ, he liked to dwell on the spiritual motherhood of Mary embracing the whole mystical body in the scene at Calvary. He sees her at the foot of the Cross. He ventures even to call her co-redemptress with her divine Son in the redemption of the world.[22] "Undoubtedly," he declares, "we owe everything to Jesus Christ, but the Mother is inseparable from the Son."[23]

In his theology lectures he developed the traditional theme of the new Eve associated with Christ in all the work of our salvation. "We must regard it as a fundamental principle that the Virgin Mother holds the same place in the scheme of the restoration of the human race as Eve held in our ruin. In fact, we know from the prophecy of Genesis that the whole economy of our salvation is based on a plan of retribution. The new Eve is associated inseparably with the new Adam."

These ideas on the cult of Our Lady which were to be so fully developed later at the instance of his illustrious friend and disciple, Cardinal Mercier, were still in the process of formation. The Abbot of Maredsous, when he became a member of the theological commission founded by the Cardinal, was asked to prepare a petition in support of the definition of the Universal Mediation of Mary. This precious document has been preserved. While all the necessary reservations are made and full weight given to them, one can detect in it the personal opinion of the theologian in favour of this title of Mary Mediatrix of all graces, a title based on her divine Motherhood, on her dignity, her power of intercession, her close association with Christ at the foot of the Cross, but recognizing her complete dependence on and subordination to the one Mediator, Christ.

[21] Sermon to the Carmel, Louvain, July 16th, 1899.
[22] Ibidem.   [23] Ibidem.

O

"Behold Your Mother"

"Devotion to Mary is not a matter of supererogation; it is essential," said Dom Marmion, "it is a direct consequence of the Incarnation."[24] "That is why those who do not know the Blessed Virgin, who do not love her, run a great risk of not understanding the mystery of the Incarnation and the other mysteries concerning the humanity of Christ. The nations who have lost their love for Mary have lost also their faith in the Incarnation. If we want to love Christ, if we want Him to be all for us and want ourselves to be all for Him, we must have a true and great devotion to the Blessed Virgin."[25]

For Dom Marmion this devotion is summed up in our realization of the part played by Mary in the life of each one of us. In his preaching, in his retreats, in his direction of souls, he repeated constantly the words of Christ on the Cross; *Ecce Mater tua*, "Behold your Mother!" These words determined for him the fundamental attitude of our tender devotion to Mary. As she is our Mother, we must, like Jesus Christ, love and venerate her with the heart of a son.

Personal intimacy with Mary

Could it be said that Dom Marmion was a "Marian" soul? He gives us the answer to this question himself like a true master of the spiritual life, and expresses, in a few terse sentences pregnant with meaning, his personal concept of devotion to Our Lady.

With a rare depth of thought he incorporates his attitude towards Mary in the glorious synthesis of our predestination in Jesus Christ according to the divine plan which constitutes the axis of our spirituality. "All our perfection consists in reproducing the image of Jesus Christ. God has predestined us to become like to His Son. *Praedestinavit nos conformes fieri imaginis Filii sui.*"[26, 27]

[24] Retreat, Louvain, November 1901.
[25] Conference, Maredret, February 1st, 1911.
[26] Rom. viii, 29.　　　　　　[27] Retreat to priests, Louvain, November 1901.

"Now, in Jesus Christ there are attributes and perfections which are fundamental and essential and others which flow from these and which we regard as secondary. As regards those attributes which are essential, every Christian must reproduce them, and their perfection in each soul is the measure of its perfection; while the other attributes of Our Lord are reproduced more or less perfectly in souls according to the circumstances and the impulse of the Holy Ghost. But there are two fundamental attributes which constitute, so to speak, the essence of the Man-God, and their imitation, their reproduction in ourselves, constitute the essence of our sanctity: Jesus is *Filius Patris* and *Filius Mariae*. The more fully we are, in Him, children of God and children of Mary, the more fully we shall share in His infinite sanctity, the more perfect we shall be. It is by Baptism that, putting on Jesus Christ, we became of necessity in Him the children of the eternal Father and the children of Mary."[28] "This is not a mere figure of speech or metaphor. As St. John says: 'It is not only in name but in very fact that we are the sons of God.'[29] In like manner we are in all reality the children of Mary, for she is the Mother of His mystical body. From the cross Jesus confided us formally to Mary, for as it was in joy that she engendered her Child who was immaculate, so it was in sorrow that she was to become the Mother of sinners."[30]

It is for us to conform to this grace of adoption by filling our hearts with the feelings which Christ Himself had for His Mother. "As Jesus Christ was by His very essence the Son of God and the Son of Mary, so we must be by grace what Jesus Christ is by nature: children of God and children of Mary. God will recognize as His true children only those who, like Jesus, are the true children of Mary."[31]

These words sum up the whole of Dom Marmion's spirit of devotion to Mary, both from the dogmatic aspect and from the fundamental Christian approach to Our Lady. They incorporate our whole spiritual life and our cult of Our Lady in the mystery of the Incarnation which effected our redemp-

---

[28] Retreat, Maredsous, September 1900.   [29] I John iii, 1.
[30] Retreat to priests, Louvain, November 1901.
[31] Sermon to the Carmel of Louvain, July 16th, 1901.

tion, and unite us inseparably to Jesus in the whole economy of our salvation. This formula of devotion to Our Lady touches on the very essentials of Christian belief and practice.

The whole object of the Christian therefore, in his devotion to Mary, must consist in taking as his model the intimate sentiments of Jesus towards His Mother. "Jesus Christ is our model. And just as we find in Him the perfect example of the child of God, so shall we find in Him too the perfect example of the child of Mary."[32]

What must we do in order to realize this sublime programme? "Jesus chose his Mother from all eternity. He has conferred on her, as well as the divine Motherhood, all the privileges which we reverence in her and which He purchased with His Blood. We likewise must freely choose Mary as our mother, rejoice at all the privileges with which she is endowed and thank God for them."[33]

"Jesus was subject to His Mother: *Erat subditus illis*.[34] Let us also obey Mary. Let us be eager to follow her counsel to imitate Jesus. Does she not say to each one of us: 'Whatsoever He shall say to you, do ye ';[35] 'This is my beloved Son, Hear ye Him.'[36]

"Jesus loved and honoured His Mother. We must honour her, love her, and find our joy in her privileges. To rejoice in the divine attributes is a very high form of love.

"Let us love Mary above all mothers. For her part, her maternal heart will always be ready to forgive us. Mary sees Jesus in each one of us."[37]

During the many retreats which he gave, Dom Marmion constantly reverted to these fundamental points. He wanted to see souls identified with Jesus in His filial sentiments towards His Mother. He liked to say the prayer of St. Gertrude: "Lord, say of me to your mother: *Ecce filius tuus*, 'Behold your Son.'" We must not omit also the closing lines of his magnificent consecration to the Blessed Trinity made at Louvain at Christmas, 1908. It is one of the most exalted

---

[32] Retreat, Maredsous, September 1900.
[33] Retreat for priests, Louvain, November 1901.
[34] Luke ii, 51.   [36] Mc. ix, 6.
[35] John ii, 5.   [37] Retreat to priests, Louvain, November 1901.

efforts of his spiritual life: "O Mary, Mother of Christ, Mother of holy love, do thou form us according to the heart of thy Son." This has the true accent of the Gospel.

Thus we say that Dom Marmion was a "Marian" soul, but in his own particular form of spirituality, which impelled him ever to seek Christ as the source and living model of all sanctity. Following His example, he wished to become a living son of Mary, to be for her another Christ.

In this matter nothing can be more significant than his reaction to the writings of Grignon de Montfort. "I know 'The secret of Mary'," he wrote in 1906. "For some souls who are drawn to it by grace this devotion is doubtless fruitful and sanctifying. But for this, one must be drawn by the grace of the Holy Spirit. For myself, I have tried it and found it a source of distraction and trouble to my soul. Fr. Faber says that at first he experienced great distaste for this devotion but that later on he received the grace to practise it with great consolation and benefit for his soul.

"In fact I do not practise it myself. I go to God through Jesus. Our Lady helps me to know her Son and to approach Him. As for other people, if they feel attracted to it, I encourage them, for this devotion has been propagated by a saint and, if it seems exaggerated to us, it may be because we are not yet at his level of sanctity."[38]

Every soul must go to God by his own way. All this in no way lessens the value of the *Treatise on true devotion to the Blessed Virgin Mary* which is the most excellent masterpiece of Marian literature in the Church and marks out what is probably the shortest way to achieve transformation into the spirit of Mary and, through her, into the spirit of Jesus Christ. The treasure of the Church lies in the admirable variety of saints. Each one gives expression in his own way to one of the aspects of the grace of Christ and His infinite plenitude.

Dom Marmion went directly to Christ for the inspiration of his devotion to Our Lady. This did not prevent him, when grace so inspired him, from identifying himself with the sentiments of Mary, from reciting the divine Office in the

[38] Letter to P. François de Sales, Louvain, July 23rd, 1906.

person of the Blessed Virgin Mary, *in persona B. M. Virginis*. He would sometimes offer up his praise and his prayers, as he tells us, in her name, just as she must have offered them herself to the eternal Father through Jesus Christ, trying to make his own her sentiments of profound adoration, of humility, and confidence and above all her joy at the thought of the triumph of her Son. " I was given light," he added, " to understand that all praise addressed to Mary comes back in all its purity to the glory of the adorable Trinity as in her Magnificat. If I consecrate myself to Mary, she will receive this oblation of myself only to offer it immediately to God."[39] "One of the best means of profiting by the holy sacrifice of the Mass," he said later to a conference of priests, " is to make our dispositions correspond to those of Mary."[40]

For contemplative souls, he recommends, as a model, Mary in her hidden life. He invites them to imitate the fidelity of the Virgin who fulfilled the whole Law, not in pharisaical spirit, but inspired wholly by love. He takes the Virgin pronouncing the *Fiat* for the Incarnation as the ideal for the religious life. In each of his retreats he devoted one conference to Our Lady, exhorting souls to live closely united to her, and in his directions he urged his penitents to turn to her: "Go to her in all your difficulties."[41]

For his own part he consecrated himself to her service every morning: "I ask her to accept me as her son: *Ecce filius tuus.*" While on a pilgrimage to Lourdes he wrote: "I am receiving great graces here."[42]

He did not like to see souls burdening themselves with too many practices of devotion. "Particular devotions are like flowers in a garden; you must know how to make a choice. One may be as good as the other. It does not matter so much which you choose, provided you are faithful to it."[43]

Apart from the Holy Sacrifice and the Office, he was particularly attached to the Rosary. "I know," he used to say, that there are liturgists who profess to despise the rosary on

---

[39] *Private Notes,* September 1888.
[40] Conference to priests, Dinant, May 1898.
[41] Letter, undated.
[42] Letter to Winefrid Kraemer, September 24th, 1922.
[43] Retreat to priests. Louvain, November 1901.

the ground that it is a devotion fit only for women and children. But if you want to enter into the kingdom of heaven you must be little: 'Unless you become as little children you shall not enter into the kingdom of heaven.'[44]   Great personages are not destined for heaven."[45]

He used to declare that the Rosary recited devoutly could lead souls to the highest perfection.

He showed rare penetration in his grasp of the essentials of this devotion. His contemplative soul was completely at ease in the vast field of the mysteries of our redemption.

"Each mystery of the life of Christ contains a secret virtue for those who meditate on it with faith and love. In the mysteries of the Rosary, as in the liturgical year, Christ is not only a model for us but a living source of sanctity. Hence the extraordinary power of this devotion to lead us to sanctity. While contemplating the mysteries we are begging the eternal Father in the name of His Son and through the intercession of Our Lady to grant us the grace to imitate the virtue exemplified by each of these mysteries in accordance with the petition of the Church in the prayer of the feast: *et imitemur quod continent.*

"What a wonderful source of grace and sanctity the Rosary is for those who practise this devotion according to its true spirit."[46]

The reason for his great affection for the Rosary was that he saw in it, as in the Liturgy, a synopsis of all the mysteries of Christ. And for him there was always the one dominating idea: Christ is everything.

If we read again in *Christ, the Life of the Soul* the splendid chapters on the Mother of the Word Incarnate, or the sublime doctrine on the hidden life of Mary in *Christ in His Mysteries* we shall understand, clearly, how inseparably the mystery of Mary was united with the mystery of Christ in the mind of Dom Marmion.

The invocation which he had chosen to introduce his conferences and which he pronounced with striking reverence is

[44] Matt. xviii, 3.
[45] Retreat, Maredsous, September 1919.
[46] Sermon, Brussels, October 1905.

expressive of the most fundamental tendency of his soul and the great passion of his life: "Mater Christi". Dom Marmion saw in Our Lady above all else the Mother of Christ. This explains the form of his devotion to Mary which was so personal and so profound. His ideal was to be for Mary another son, *alter Christus*.

THE DOCTRINE OF OUR VOCATION OF ADOPTION

All sanctity consists in being by grace what Jesus is by nature: the child of God.

EPILOGUE

THE DOCTRINE OF OUR VOCATION OF ADOPTION

I n centering his spiritual doctrine around Christ, Dom Marmion has gone to the very heart of Christianity. And in Christ he went straight to the very root of the mystery, to His divine Sonship, which is the source and model of our own. Other authors before him have expounded the splendour of our grace of adoption; he stands out by having built on it the whole of his spiritual doctrine. We have here the inspiration, the dominating idea, and the point of convergence of all his thought.

This privileged status of children of God clothes Christians in an infinite grandeur by their participation in the eternal Sonship of the Word, and this grace of adoption is the source of our sanctity, just as the hypostatic union was for Jesus the source of all grace and all gifts. Our spiritual life takes on from this a new meaning: it is in each one of us an extension of the Incarnation of the Word which raises all the members of the mystical body to the personal dignity of the Son of God. St. Thomas Aquinas goes so far as to speak of "the one mystical personality", *quasi una persona mystica*.[1] By having seen this in all its simplicity and depth; by having made of it, not by any rigorous systematizing, but in a spontaneous and vital spirit, the centre point of his aspirations and teaching, he has won for himself in the history of spiritual doctrine the title of Doctor of the divine adoption.

The varied aspects of his work are brought together in a striking unity. It is in the bosom of the Father that he con-

---

[1] *Summa* III, xlviii, 2 ad 1; and elsewhere: Tota Ecclesia quae est mysticum *corpus Christi, computatur quasi una persona cum suo capite, quod est Christus.* III, xlix, 1.

templates our spiritual life in its eternal origins. His conception of our sanctity is extended by these infinite horizons. The
Father communicates all His divinity to the Son by way of
eternal generation. He has bestowed on the Humanity of
Jesus the fulness of grace which is extended to all the members of His mystical body according as they are willing to
receive it by faith and love. Man is destined to participate in
the divine Sonship: "predestined to be made conformable to
the image of His Son."[2] This divine plan is the key to the
whole mystery: "Behold what manner of charity the Father
hath bestowed on us that we should be called and should be
the sons of God."[3] "This is the explanation of all the mercies
of God towards us; it is the source of all graces and the very
essence of the Christian life."[4]

The grace of our adoption is therefore inseparable from the
eternal Sonship of Christ. The Word Incarnate is the exemplary, the meritorious and the efficient cause, of our predestination. It is this supreme intuition derived from his reading of
St. Paul which illuminates, as it were, from above, Dom Marmion's whole vision of the universe. It is only His Son whom
God sees in men. He would have them like to Him, and their
perfection varies according to their degree of conformity to
Christ.

"We receive the grace of adoption on the day of our
Baptism":[5] this grace of Sonship is developed in us by Confirmation and the other sacraments; the Eucharist effects the
final stage on this earth by imprinting on our souls the characteristics of Jesus Christ.

The whole of his teaching is inspired by this noble dogmatic
perspective. If it can be said that our concept of God dominates our whole moral life, then we may say that the axis of his
spiritual doctrine was constituted by the two correlative
truths, the divine paternity and the filial spirit. "We are the
children of God by adoption. Our relations with Him must
be those of a child with his Father."[6] We are children of God,

[2] Rom. viii, 29.   [3] I John iii, 1.
[4] Conference to priests, Dinant, July 1897.
[5] Retreat, Maredret, February 1914.
[6] *Private Notes*, Feast of the Sacred Heart, 1887.

perfect Christians in as far as we imitate Christ. And we find in his notes this revealing equation;

" Saint = child of God."

A saint is one "who has allowed the grace of adoption to develop in his soul."[7] "All sanctity consists in being by grace what Jesus is by nature: a child of God."[8]

Such is the vast synthesis of spiritual doctrine which Dom Marmion has left to the Church. He has led us back to the Gospels, to St. Paul and to the mysticism of the early Christians. God the Father has sent us His Only-begotten Son to make us His children by adoption. Our souls must return to the Father by the Son in the Holy Spirit. There is no other way. It is Christ who leads us *in sinu Patris;*[9] and there, with Him and in Him, in His spirit, we can say to God in the same accents of filial affection: "ABBA! FATHER!"[10]

---

[7] Conference, Maredret, June 1914.
[8] Retreat, Hayward's Heath, August 1906.

[9] I John i, 18.
[10] Rom. viii, 15.